HARRIER

Series Editor : Christopher Chant

Foulis

Titles in the *Super Profile* series:

Boeing 707

B-29 Superfortress

Harrier

Further titles in this series will be published at regular intervals. For information on new titles please contact your bookseller or write to the publisher.

ISBN 0 85429 357 4

A FOULIS Aircraft Book

First published 1983

Published by:
Haynes Publishing Group
Sparkford,
Yeovil,
Somerset BA22 7JJ

Distributed in North America by:
Haynes Publications Inc.
861 Lawrence Drive,
Newbury Park,
California 91320, USA

Produced by:
Winchmore Publishing Services Limited,
40 Triton Square,
London NW1

Edited by Catherine Bradley
Designed by Andrzej Bielecki
Picture research Jonathan Moore
Printed in Hong Kong by Lee Fung Asco Limited.

Contents

The extensive but still growing **Harrier** family is now more than 20 years old, and is still unique among the world's air arms. The feature that makes the Harrier unique is its ability to take-off and land vertically (VTOL) or, to increase payload, to take-off after only a very short run and later land vertically (V/STOL). For two decades this revolutionary feature has been demonstrated to civilians and military alike in air shows and on other occasions, but it is true to say that the Harrier represents an amazing combination of the radical and the conventional in military technology, which has only recently come to be appreciated fully.

Even during World War II it was a favourite tactic (inherited from the relatively primitive efforts of World War I) to defeat enemy air power where it was most vulnerable: stationary on their airfields, aircraft were easy prey for bombs, rockets and gunfire. Just as significantly, the runways so vital for conventional aircraft operations could be cratered to render the airfields inoperative until much time and effort had been expended on filling in the craters. This latter tactic was increasingly significant in the closing stages of World War II as heavier aircraft with more critical field performance came to demand longer (and hence more vulnerable) runways, often built

of concrete. Such airfields were costly to build and repair, for it was impossible to conceal them from chance passers-by, let alone specially equipped photographic reconnaissance aircraft at high altitude. This tactically inhibiting factor became more and more prominent in the early 1950s, as the widespread adoption of first- and second-generation jet-propelled aircraft became the norm for air arms with any pretensions to sophistication. With pious optimism, the member nations of the NATO alliance littered much of western Europe with horribly visible and vulnerable concrete airstrips whose defence was 'assured' by large numbers of medium- and large-

calibre cannon. This 'assurance' was complemented by equally impressive quantities of expensive repair equipment. Such a system might have been effective against the type of attack mounted in World War II, but it was gradually seen to be useless against the threat posed by the growing arsenal of short- and medium-range missiles, many with nuclear warheads, deployed for such tactical purposes by the USSR, whose offensive ambitions NATO had been formed to counter. Then the fact had to be accepted (but was carefully ignored by most NATO countries) that such missiles posed a decisive threat to conventional air power: there was no defence against such missiles, and the damage inflicted on any airfield by one such weapon would be irreparable in tactical timescales.

As is so often the case in such circumstances, there was much discussion of the problem, but it was accompanied by very little effort. There was much talk of dispersed activity in times in crisis, with tactical aircraft operating from lengths of road and the like, but such discussions ignored that the aircraft were not designed for such primitive operating conditions, and that the air forces lacked the personnel, training, equipment and transport to sustain such operations in the field. Only two nations, both outside the NATO alliance, actually acted to meet the threat: Switzerland instituted an enormous programme of cavern-building, with huge hangars and maintenance facilities hewn into mountainsides; and Sweden began to develop combat aircraft with short take-off and landing (STOL) performance that could operate with the aid of specially trained and equipped detachments from large numbers of short, and thus not easily destroyed, lengths of road.

In typical pose: a Harrier GR. Mk 3 (built originally as a GR. Mk 1) hovers over a German cornfield while on detachment with No. 3 Squadron, usually based at RAF Gütersloh. Well displayed are the twin ventral cannon pads, which double as strakes to trap gases and so improve the hover performance.

Harrier T Mk 4

H HYDRAULICS

H1 Nitrogen bottle (u/c and air brake emergenc operation)
H2 General service system hand pump and press gauge
H3 Ground servicing points No.1 system
H4 Reservoir No.1 system
H5 Accumulator, nose wheel steering

STRUCTURE

1 Pitot probe
2 Detachable nosecone
3 Front pressure bulkhead
4 Pressure floor
5 Martin-Baker Type 9D Mk.1 Ejection Seat
6 Machined windscreen frame and arch
7 Bird-proof windscreen
8 Bird-proof stretched acrylic quarter lights
9 Manually operated canopy (Front)
10 Manually operated canopy (Rear)
11 Miniature detonating cord
12 Unstretched acrylic canopy
13 Unstretched acrylic canopy
14 Machined nose-gear/keel beams
15 Boundary air bleed doors (suction operated)
16 Bleed-air duct to outlet aft of rear canopy
17 Free-floating intake suction relief
18 Extruded L-section longeron
19 Z-section stringers
20 Fabricated front engine mounting frame
21 Machined main gear beams
22 Machined bulkhead
23 Rear fuselage access
24 Mainplane attachment (mainplane removed for engine removal)
25 Mainplane attachment link to rear spar
26 Front spar web
27 Centre spar web
28 Rear spar web
29 Skin lap-joint
30 Lap-joint (top skin only)
31 Etched outer skin panel
32 Riveted rolled stringers (outer panel)
33 Rolled section outer spar
34 Machined sub-spar
35 Machined skin plank
36 Machined rib
37 Plastic bumper
38 Bonded aluminium honeycomb structure
39 Windscreen wash tank
40 Camera
41 Footstep
42 Rear valve heat shield
43 Ballast weights
44 Ventral fin attachment to Fr.43
45 Retractable footstep

P POWERPLANT

P1 Forward throttle and nozzle controls
P2 Throttle control rods
P3 First-stage fan blades
P4 Engine oil pressure filler
P5 Engine oil pressure filler access
P6 Fan casing
P7 Fan air duct
P8 Fan air nozzle
P9 Gas turbine exhaust nozzle
P10 Rear nozzle bearings cooling air
P11 Zone One venting air
P12 Venting airflow induction air (engine bleed)
P13 Zone Two venting air
P14 Compensating rear engine support
P15 Water injection tank
P16 Fire suppression spray ring
P17 Dual wall hose
P18 Nozzle rotation air-motors
P19 Gearbox
P20 Drive shaft to rear nozzles
P21 Drive to front nozzles
P22 Chain and sprocket to nozzle

F FUEL SYSTEM

F1 Port front tank
F2 Port centre tank
F3 Rear fuselage tank
F4 Tank end rib, integral port wing tank
F5 Tank pressurising air
F6 Booster pump and inverted flight valve
F7 In-flight refuelling valve (for detachable probe)
F8 In-flight refuelling line
F9 Refuelling valve
F10 Ground refuelling point
F11 Refuelling warning lights and switches
F12 Defuelling valve
F13 To fuel delivery line
F14 L.p.cock (from proportioner to engine via flowmete
F15 L.p.cock control
F16 Transfer line
F17 External tank transfer
F18 Fuel tank float-switch
F19 Jettison valve
F20 Jettison pipe

J UNDERCARRIAGE

U1 Rigid live-axle mounted mainwheel
U2 Multi-disc brakes
U3 Retraction jack
U4 Pre-shortening nose-gear leg
U5 Liquid Spring unit
U6 Steering motor plus or minus 45 deg.
 (179 deg. disengaged)
U7 Steering control valve
U8 Outrigger wheels (180 deg. castor inwards only)
U9 Leg pivot
U10 Pre-closing door
U11 Door jacks

E ELECTRONICS & ELECTRICS

E1 Nav/attack display
E2 Nav/attack computer
E3 Sight and head-up display
E4 Shockproof equipment rack with integral cooling
 duct carries Tacan, IFF, U/VHF radio. Lower
 rack air data, nav/attack equipment.
E5 Transformer-rectifier unit
E6 VHF aerial
E7 HF notch aerial
E8 IFF aerial blade
E9 UHF stand-by aerial
E10 Tacan aerial
E11 Batteries, 28V 25AH
E12 Cable duct
E13 Landing lamps
E14 Nav. lights
E15 Ground intercom socket
F16 HF Tuner
E17 Impedance matching unit HF aerial
E18 Anti-collision light

C CONTROL SYSTEMS

C1 Rudder input from pedals
C2 Rudder quadrant
C3 Rudder cable tensioner
C4 Rudder centring unit
C5 Linkage from rudder to
 Yaw Reaction Control Valve (RCV)
C6 Tailplane control unpit from column
C7 Tailplane quadrant
C8 Tandem tailplane jack
C9 Linkage to pitch RCV
C10 Pitch spring feel
C1J Pitch Q-feel
C12 Aileron control rod
C13 Tandem aileron jack with autostabiliser
C14 Aileron offset hinge
C15 Reaction control bleed air supply shut-off valve
 (Fully open after 20 deg. nozzle rotation)
C16 Duct to roll RCV
C17 Duct to pitch RCV
C18 Duct to pitch and yaw RCV
C19 Control cable and pipe run duct
C20 Rudder and tailplane cables
C21 Nose up pitch RCV
C22 Nose down pitch and yaw RCV
C23 Roll RCV
C24 Airbrake
C25 Airbrake jack
C26 Tailplane compensator
C27 Torque shaft for yaw RCV
C28 Front RCV input and inertial weight
C29 Tailplane vibration dampers

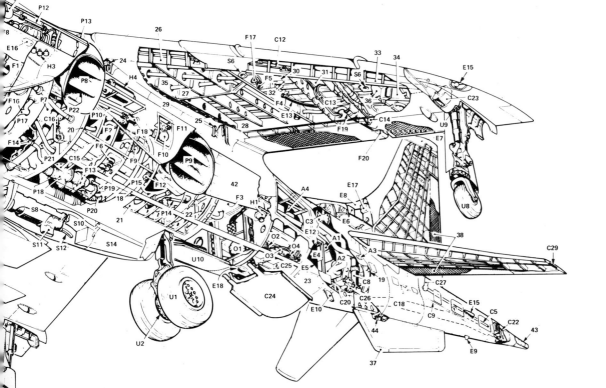

S STORES

S STORES

S1 M.L. twin store carrier
S2 Outer pylon
S3 E.R.U. cartridges
S4 Armament relay box access
S5 Nose fusing connectors
S6 Pylon mounting points
S7 30mm. Aden gun pod
S8 30mm. Aden gun
S9 Blast suppressor ports
S10 Feed
S11 Case ejection
S12 Link ejection
S13 Frangible cap
S14 Ammunition box (100 rounds)

A AIR SYSTEMS

A AIR SYSTEMS

A1 Heat exchanger ⎤
A2 Cold air unit ⎟ Equipment
A3 Ram air exhaust ⎟ Cooling
A4 Delivery to racks ⎦ System
A5 Cockpit ram air exhaust
A6 Water extractor
A7 Foot warm air
A8 Quarter light demisting air
A9 Canopy de-misting air
A10 Cockpit air conditioning duct

O OXYGEN

O OXYGEN

O1 Five-litre lox container
O2 Build-up coil
O3 Ground charging point
O4 Pressure gauge

Genesis

Far-sighted designers had appreciated the problems associated with reliance on runways for some time, and several radical alternatives had been proposed. Some, such as the Focke-Wulf Triebflügel of World War II, were probably too advanced for current technology: the Triebflügel, which did not advance beyond the concept stage, was a rotary-wing tail-sitter whose three wings revolved on a fuselage-mounted ball race under the power of tip-mounted ramjets. Others, such as the Bachem Ba 349 Natter, actually reached the hardware stage: the Natter, designed as a point interceptor, was launched vertically by a battery of solid-propellant rockets and was intended as a semi-expendable machine, the only portion of the machine intended to be reused being the cockpit section, which was to be lowered to the ground by parachutes after the sortie. After the end of World War II the Americans made some useful strides, fearing that their aircraft-carriers would be unable to accommodate useful numbers of conventional take-off aircraft: thus were born the Convair XFY-1 and Lockheed XFV-1 turboprop-powered tail-sitters, which both encountered intractable problems with low-speed control. Another tail-sitting design was the French Zborowski Coleoptère, but by the mid-1950s most designers (with the notable exception of Rolls-Royce, which continued to exhibit a touching faith in direct vertical lift with the aid of massed batteries of lift-jets) had come to the conclusion that a different approach was necessary before the concept of VTOL could be realised as a practical possibility.

A first step in that direction was the Bell VTO of 1954, which was powered by a pair of J44 turbojets mounted on the sides of the fuselage at the centre of gravity position. These could be swivelled to the vertical position to lift the aircraft from the ground, and then slowly turned to the horizontal position to propel the aircraft into level flight where lift was provided by the wings. The concept was developed with the Bell X-14, which again mounted a pair of turbojets on the sides of the fuselage. The X-14 had Bristol Siddeley Vipers, installed in fixed horizontal positions but fitted with tailpipe deflectors on the centre of gravity to turn the jet thrust through 90° for VTOL operations. While the VTO can be considered a swivelling-thrust machine, the X-14 was a true vectored-thrust aircraft, and thus the real precursor of today's most effective VTOL system for fixed-wing aircraft.

These first VTOL aircraft were nothing more than research platforms, intended to investigate the phenomenon of vertical take-off and landing. But then the pioneer French designer Michel Wibault combined the known vulnerability of NATO airfields with VTOL technology to produce a design for a VTOL aircraft intended for combat operations. This was the Wibault Gyroptère of 1956. Intended as a ground-attack fighter, the Gyroptère was a mid-wing monoplane with small flying surfaces and a portly fuselage. In its exterior design and concept there was little remarkable in this swept-wing design. What was remarkable was the powerplant: an 8,000-hp (5,968-kW) Bristol Orion turbo-prop located in the rear fuselage and designed to drive, instead of the normal tractor propeller, four massive centrifugal compressors that exhausted through rotating scrolls located two on each side of the lower fuselage, the pair on each side being located equi-distantly fore and aft of the centre of gravity. For VTO the scrolls were rotated so that the efflux was directed vertically downwards and for transition to wing-borne flight the scrolls were slowly turned aft to the horizontal position to develop forward thrust.

Careful examination of the Gyroptère confirmed the general soundness of VTOL for combat operations in the European theatre, but also the mechanical inefficiency of the Wibault turbine/compressor combination. This conclusion was reached by the Mutual Weapons Development Program (MWDP), a US-sponsored body advising on increased weapons development within the European NATO countries, and by the NATO Advisory Group for Aeronautical Research and Development (AGARD). Particularly important in the evaluation was the involve-ment of Dr. Stanley Hooker, the technical director of Bristol and lately of Rolls-Royce, brought into the assessment panel by Colonel Willis Chapman of the MWDP. Hooker appreciated that the Wibault design offered a unique trio of benefits: single-engine VTOL capability in a flat-rising design that had no need to transition from the vertical to the horizontal position for wing-borne flight; single-system lift and propulsion layout thanks to the use of vectoring nozzles; and a balanced lift system disposed adequately round the centre of gravity to ease control problems. Hooker also appreciated the mechanical disadvantages of the Wibault system, and so brought in Gordon Lewis of Bristol to improve the layout. Lewis, in just a fortnight, evolved a considerably more refined powerplant desig-nated Bristol BE.48, with the Orion driving by means of a reduction gearbox (instead of Wibault's bevelled units, one to each pair of compressors) a fan comprising the first two stages of the Bristol Olympus turbojet; this fan delivered cold air to just two

8

nozzles, which again could be vectored through 90° for lift and then propulsion. Lewis kept up the good work and soon turned the BE.48 into the BE.53 by the simple replacement of the Orion by the lighter but equally powerful Orpheus turbojet, driving the front fan by means of a low-pressure trailing turbine with its shaft running through the inside of the high-pressure shaft of the Orpheus gas generator. This eliminated the need for the weighty gearbox, the turbine in the jet efflux being matched ideally to the front fan. Anticipated thrust was 8,000 lb (3,629 kg), and a VTOL combat aircraft with a useful payload would have needed two such engines, which would have provided the ideal four nozzles disposed around the centre of gravity.

It was a workable system, but Hooker failed to interest the Ministry of Supply in London, for there was no official RAF require-

ment for a VTOL aircraft, and such service interest as existed was centred on the use of batteries of Rolls-Royce lift engines. This alternative to vectored thrust had strong backing at the time, despite the clear disadvantage of the system: for though such a VTOL aircraft, with separate lift and propulsion engines, avoided the mechanical complexity of vectored thrust, it had to carry in wing-borne flight a heavy battery of unused engines, reducing payload and offering a greater target for critical damage in combat.

A series of official meetings failed to produce anything but quantities of paper, so Hooker took the sensible decision to deal directly with Hawker Aircraft, the main supplier of light aircraft to the RAF. Hooker was encouraged in his approach by the fact that head of design at Hawker was Sir Sydney Camm, doyen of British fighter designers and in his time not averse to technological

development. However, in 1957 Camm was deeply involved in the design of the Hawker **P.1121**, a Mach 2 fighter intended to succeed the legendary Hawker Hunter in RAF service, so the Bristol proposal was passed to Ralph Hooper. In the event this was probably fortunate, for Camm later came to distrust the V/STOL concept as too risky, the lives of air crew coming first in Camm's design procedure. Camm himself became involved in the V/STOL project after the cancellation of the P.1121 in the wake of the infamous 1957 White Paper that forecast the demise of manned military aircraft in favour of missiles. Camm's main interest was an ultimately vain effort to turn the P.1121 into a twin-engine **P.1129**, but he authorised Hooper to pursue the V/STOL concept.

The fourth new-built Harrier GR. Mk 3 is on the strength of No. 4 Squadron, NATO-declared at Gütersloh in West Germany.

Hawker P.1127

The problem facing Hooper and his colleague John Fozard was formidable, because the BE.53 proposal had only two nozzles. This meant that in a single-engine design the vectoring nozzles had to be turned to blast forward as well as downward, so as to cancel the forward thrust of the hot gases from the core engine. Moreover, the designs of the vectoring nozzles and their fairings were still rudimentary, and as a result Hooper's initial **P.1127** scheme was nearer a research machine than an aircraft with military potential: an unswept mid-wing monoplane with the BE.53 buried in the fuselage under the wing, fed through a chin inlet below the extensively glazed cockpit for the two crew and exhausting the hot gases from a ventral nozzle aft of the wing trailing edge and the vectored cold gas through nozzles on the centre of gravity at about one-third of the chord. This design was soon evolved into a more practical machine with lateral inlets, but still not capable of VTOL with the BE.53. The prospects for the aircraft looked dismal — but so too did the prospects for Hawker, and work was pushed forward for lack of anything else.

The breakthrough came with an idea from Fozard: if the tail-pipe for the hot gases were bifurcated (in the fashion already adopted for the Hawker Sea Hawk), it might then be possible to add an extra pair of vectoring nozzles and use the whole of the powerplant's output for VTOL purposes. Fozard capped this inspiration with the notion that a blind of cascades in each nozzle would facilitate the angling of the gases, and so permit smaller, lighter nozzles with less drag and installation difficulty. Bristol were not impressed at first with

The serial XP972 identifies this aircraft as the third P.1127 aircraft, extensively used for the development of the Fairey control system. The aircraft was heavily damaged after a forced landing during September 1962 after Hugh Merewether saw a fire-warning light over Tangmere. The landing gear failed to sustain the landing impetus and the aircraft caught fire. The cause of the problem was later determined as an engine main bearing failure, which caused the compressor to disintegrate, blowing a hole in the side of the compressor casing. *Left:* The Pegasus vectored-thrust engine.

Hawker's intrusion into the powerplant field, and this feeling was enhanced when Hawker suggested that the low- and high-pressure spools of the engine could be arranged to rotate in opposite directions to reduce torque, which the aircraft designers rightly appreciated would present difficult control problems for the P.1127 in the hovering mode. Slowly the differences between the two concerns were eliminated, and towards the middle of 1957 Bristol had recast the BE.53 design to include contra-rotating low- and high-pressure spools. An input from Bristol that also helped transmogrify the engine was the provision of a common

inlet for the whole powerplant, so that the compressed gas from the fan was fed also to the core engine, effectively supercharging the latter. With four vectoring nozzles, the revised engine was designated BE.53/2, and was prospectively rated at a thrust of 9,000 lb (4,082 kg). This was the engine for which Hawker had been waiting, and the Hooper design began to move rapidly towards the definitive P.1127 configuration, with nozzles arranged round the centre of gravity to provide 'four-poster' lift and permit VTOL.

Hawker were able to move ahead slowly with only a small capital expenditure, but Bristol were faced with a financial

problem of greater magnitude as further progress called for a prototype engine. Early in 1958 the company decided that such an expenditure could not be met by Bristol alone. Into the breach stepped the MWDP, which offered to provide three-quarters of the necessary funding, leaving Bristol to find only one-quarter. Despite escalating costs, the initial target of six prototype engines was met, and the first of these, by now named Pegasus 1, ran in September 1959.

In March 1959 Hawker Siddeley, as the company had by then become, decided to build, as a private venture, two prototype P.1127s. In 1958 the P.1127 had reached its definitive aero-

dynamic form, and during the year great effort went into the design of an ancillary system essential to the success of the whole project: the reaction control system to stabilise the aircraft at speeds below those at which the conventional flight controls would work. Hooper's first thought was to use cold gas bled from the two-stage fan of the definitive engine through simply manufactured aluminium piping. But then Hooper realised that to carry a sufficient volume of gas the piping would have to have a diameter too great to fit inside the wing for the lateral controls. Hooper thus came to the conclusion that hot gases would have to be bled from the

high-pressure spool, and carried in stainless-steel piping. A system of continuous bleed was selected, feeding downward-blowing reaction control valves at the wingtips and at the nose and tail, the latter being trainable laterally for yaw control. One of the features that finally made the P.1127 so distinctive was the landing gear, which was fixed as tandem main units under the fuselage (with twin wheels on the rear unit and a single wheel on the front leg), with retractable outrigger units at the wingtips for balance on the ground.

Soon after Hawker Siddeley had committed themselves to the manufacture of the two proto-types, which the company

unofficially suggested as the basis for a light ground-attack machine, NATO announced the compe-tition for a V/STOL aircraft under the NATO Basic Military Require-ment Three (NBMR-3) specifi-cation. In the light of this quasi-official requirement for an aircraft to succeed the Fiat G.91 series, the British government finally began to take a slight (but only slight) interest in the Hawker design and the Bristol engine. There was minimal official stimulus for the P.1127 project, but Hawker Siddeley were further encouraged by the success of Bristol with the Pegasus, which had by February 1960 run in the Pegasus 2 (BE.53/3) form rated at 11,000-lb (4,990-kg) thrust,

The first P.1127, with 'Bill' Bedford at the controls, makes an early tethered essay into the air. Note the wool tufts on the rear fuselage (for airflow determination), the quartered camera targets and the unfaired outrigger legs.

with a core based on the Orpheus 6 rather than the earlier Orpheus 3 to provide the bleed gas for the reaction control system, all of whose effluxes were directed downwards to supplement the thrust of the vectoring nozzles.

Much thought was devoted to the problems of control as the P.1127 accelerated from hovering to wing-borne flight, and Hawker Siddeley were fortunate in continued American support, which permitted the wind-tunnel testing of models by NASA and the use of various American research aircraft by Hawker Siddeley test pilots as familiarisation vehicles for the eventual P.1127 programme.

British official favour came in February 1962, when the Ministry of Supply agreed to cover the costs of the two P.1127 prototypes, which were allocated the official serials XP831 and XP836 as research aircraft. The work progressed rapidly in the Hawker Siddeley experimental shops, and the first P.1127 was completed in the late summer of 1960. It was appreciated that VTOL performance would be marginal, and all extra items were removed from the aircraft, bell-mouth inlets were fitted to increase the airflow into the Pegasus, and on 21 October 1960 Hawker Siddeley's chief test pilot, A. W. 'Bill' Bedford, made the first flight: the aircraft was tethered by its nose leg and outriggers to weights under a metal grid under the aircraft, and intercom wires running into the small ventral fin gave the appearance that the P.1127 was tethered at all four corners. It was a small beginning, but the world's first practical V/STOL aircraft with vectored thrust had flown. Though there was little that was entirely new in the P.1127, it was the first time that all the components of a practical vectored-thrust V/STOL aircraft had been put into a single machine that had the potential of

XP980 was the penultimate P.1127, and introduced streamwise tips, anhedral on a larger tailplane, and the pressure-trapping ventral strakes.

being more than a pure research machine, despite the strictures of the British government.

Tests proceeded well, if not smoothly, because it soon became apparent that the tethers adversely affected the stability of the aircraft in the air, and that the reaction control valves at the nose and tail were wholly inadequate to keeping the aircraft from turning tail-on to the wind. Tests were restricted to the hovering mode, and a crucial date was 19 November 1960, when the tethers were finally removed and the P.1127 XP831 hovered in free flight for the first time, immediately displaying far greater controlability in the air. With the hovering tests complete, it was appreciated that conventional flight must also be essayed, but first there had to be trials for a number of modifications to improve the basic aircraft. The most important of these was in the system for yaw control at low speeds. The continuous-bleed process was abandoned, and in its place was fitted an intermittent-bleed system, controlled by the rudder pedals, to feed fixed reaction control valves (left and right) in the tail. Taxi trials also revealed a number of shortcomings in the landing gear, notably shimmy in the outriggers

and inadequate steering in the nosewheel. Slowly the problems were ironed out, and the virtually rebuilt XP831 was ready for flight trials in early 1961. The aircraft was moved by road to the Royal Aircraft Establishment at Bedford, and 'Bill' Bedford made the first conventional take-off there on 13 March, no flaps being used and lift-off being made at some 175 mph (282 km/h). The test programme picked up momentum in July with the delivery of the second prototype, XP836, which differed from XP831 principally in having sharp-lipped inlets for high-speed flight. The availability of two aircraft allowed the one remaining major hurdle in the flight test programme, transitions to and from horizontal flight, to be approached from two direction: XP831 was used for VTOs and transitions into forward flight and speeds of up to 105 mph (169 km/h), and XP836 was used for high-speed flight with velocity dropping from the transonic region to 105 mph (169 km/h). By September 1961 each aircraft had completed its particular aspect of the programme, and on 12 September Bedford and Hugh Merewether each completed successful transitions into and out of horizontal flight. The two test pilots now began to explore the full flight envelope with great assurance, and the speed range of the P.1127 soon ranged from backwards at some 25 mph (42 km/h) to forwards at about Mach 1 (reached in December 1961), and to Mach 1.2 in a shallow dive (reached later in December 1961).

That the government as well as the manufacturers was pleased with progress was indicated by the award of a contract during late 1960 for the production of another four P.1127 prototypes, which were regarded more as development aircraft than as research aircraft, at last providing some evidence that official interest was being given to the design as a military vehicle. However, with the NATO declaration of the NBMR-3 specification for a V/STOL ground-attack fighter in March 1961, both the British government and Camm's design team veered slightly away from development of the P.1127 as a military prototype towards more ambitious thoughts of supersonic V/STOL fighters of considerably more advanced concept, with further work on the P.1127/Pegasus combination directed towards its use as a training or conversion type pending the development of the NBMR-3 fighter.

However, Peter Thornycroft, secretary of state at the newly formed Ministry of Aviation, did not agree with the move. Thornycroft had considerable faith in the future of the P.1127 basic design in its own right, and in this belief he was confirmed by continued American interest and involvement in the design, though this was concerned primarily with the engine technology, which was making great strides in a field left vacant by American technology. As early as 1959 the Air Staff had issued Operational Requirement 345, designed to elicit proposals as to how far the P.1127 concept

could be taken, and as to the roles that might be undertaken by the design. This OR.345 was cancelled in 1962 as the Air Staff was increasingly of the opinion (wholly erroneous as events in Vietnam and various Arab-Israeli wars were to prove) that future combat aircraft had to possess Mach 2 performance. But on 14 January 1961 came further proof of genuine interest in V/STOL military aircraft, when Thornycroft announced that the British and Federal German governments were about to begin talks on the joint development of a light strike fighter based on the P.1127. Spurred by this announcement, the USA indicated that it wished to partake, initially in a tripartite evaluation squadron equipped with aircraft of the P.1127 type and financed jointly by the three countries. As so often happens in British military matters, however, the Ministry of Aviation and the RAF were not on the same wavelength, and what emerged was that while the RAF had its sights set firmly on a supersonic V/STOL aircraft, the Ministry of Aviation, Federal Germany, the USA and, perhaps Italy were more interested in a short-term operational development of the P.1127.

This last had been made feasible by the latest development in the Pegasus story. By the time of the initial P.1127 hovering trials in 1960 the Pegasus 2 had been uprated to 12,000-lb (5,443-kg) thrust, but it was clear that this offered only marginal performance and that greater thrust was necessary to permit further evolution. Bristol's response was the Pegasus 3, which first ran in April 1961 and made its initial flight just 12 months later. Compared with its predecessor, the Pegasus 3 had a revised high-pressure spool with an eighth stage to the compressor and a second stage to the turbine. Bench tests confirmed a rating of 13,500 lb (6,124 kg), soon raised to 14,000 lb

(6,350 kg), and later modifications were effected in light of test flight experiences. The first of these was the loss of XP836 on 14 December 1961, when Bedford had to eject when this second prototype entered an uncontrollable roll as he tried to land after the port front nozzle came off: the cure was found to involve the replacement of the GRP (glassfibre-reinforced plastics) front nozzles with steel units. The second was the crash, with considerable damage, of the third P.1127 (XP972) when a titanium fire resulted from the rubbing of the compressor blades on the casing during high-g manoeuvres on 30 October 1962; a fix was found in the strengthening of the casing.

The Pegasus 3 was fitted to the last three P.1127s, and permitted these three aircraft to undertake, between 1963 and 1965, the exhaustive test programme that validated the concept of V/STOL aircraft as practical military aircraft rather than temperamental research platforms. Much aerodynamic refinement went into these last three P.1127 types, including a number of universally unsuccessful inflatable rubber lips for the inlets to try to reconcile the differing requirements for V/STOL (thick-lipped) and high-speed (thin-lipped) flight. Although the inflation system in itself worked well enough, in high-speed flight the rubber of the inlet lips tended to flutter in the airstream and tear; the whole concept was finally abandoned as unworkable, and ultimately proved superfluous as the higher rating of later engines removed the need for the better airflow provided by the inflated lips. Other refinements tested were Küchemann low-drag wingtips, very slightly kinked leading edges, revisions to the outrigger configuration, altered reaction control valve housings, differently shaped inlets and a larger tailplane with anhedral.

Right: Perhaps the single most important contribution to the Harrier family's effectiveness as a close-support weapon is the Ferranti-provided moving-map display. This works on inputs from the attitude platform, Tacan, present-position computer and pilot to present an extremely accurate picture of location and heading, so allowing the pilot to make blind first-pass attacks with confidence and accuracy.

Below: With the close-support mission in mind, the designers provided the Harrier with this sharply angled cockpit offering no rearward view.

Previous page: A classic shot of the Sea Harrier FRS. Mk 1 in a tight turn. Note the spanwise vortex generators on the upper surfaces of the wing, and the small dielectric nose cone for the advanced Blue Fox radar.

Above: Sea Harrier FRS. Mk 1 aircraft of the Fleet's Air Arm's three operating squadrons. From right to left these are No. 800 Squadron, embarked on HMS *Hermes*; No. 801 Squadron, embarked on HMS *Invincible*; and No. 899 Squadron, based at the RNAS Yeovilton (HMS *Heron*).

Left: A Sea Harrier FRS. Mk 1 lines up at the rear of HMS *Invincible*'s short flight-deck for a rolling take-off. Note the shallow-angle (limited to 7° by the centre-line Sea Dart surface-to-air missile installation) 'ski-jump' that helps to project the Sea Harrier up into the air at the crucial lift-off moment.

Right: A Harrier hovers on the rear of HMS *Ark Royal*'s flightdeck during 1971. Such trials were universally successful, even on wooden flightdecks. Note *Ark Royal*'s normal complement of Phantoms and Buccaneers at the forward end of the flightdeck, and the second Harrier along-side the island.

Below: A Sea Harrier FRS. Mk 1 about to lift off HMS *Hermes*, the ski-jump permitting a rolling take-off with underwing drop tanks and Sidewinder air-to-air missiles.
Right: Flight operations on board HMS *Hermes*. Note the planeguard helicopter off the port quarter.

Above: XW927 was the last Harrier
T. Mk 2 to be built, and was subsequently
upgraded to T. Mk 4 standard. Note the
elegant revision of the forward fuselage to
seat two in tandem, and the extension of
the tailcone together with an enlargement
of the vertical tail.

Right: A Harrier GR. Mk 3 ripple-fires a
salvo of 68-mm (2.68-in) SNEB unguided
rockets from its quartet of underwing
Matra launch pods. Though relatively
inaccurate, such salvoes are quite
devastating when they hit their targets.

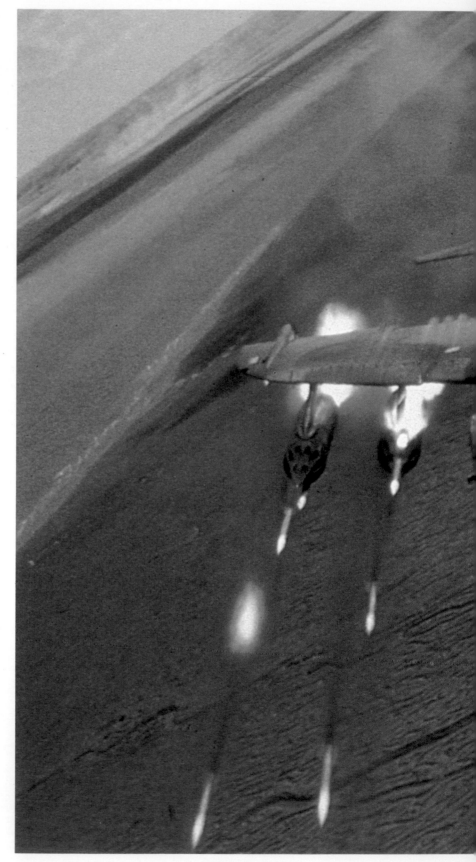

Above: A Harrier GR. Mk 1 fires rockets from the launcher on its starboard inner pylon. Note the width of the fuselage in the area of the forward nozzles.
Right: A Harrier GR. Mk 1 of No. 4 Squadron during a training mission. This unit was the second Harrier squadron, and was based at the time at RAF Wildenrath as part of RAF Germany.
Left: Accompanied by its characteristic miasma of turbulent gas and dust, a Harrier GR. Mk 3 of No. 4 Squadron lifts off without underwing stores.
Below: Sea Harrier powerplant installation.

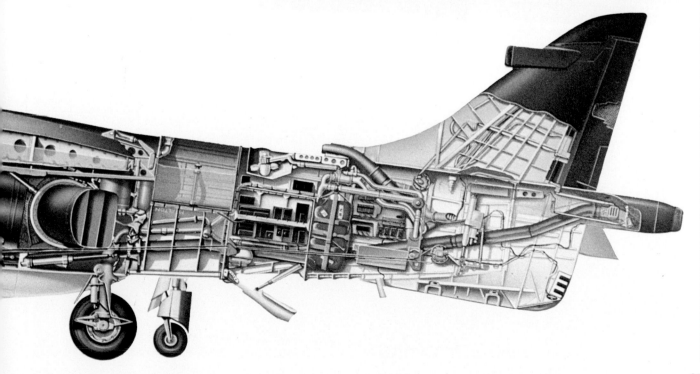

Above: Key to the capabilities of the Harrier family is the Pegasus engine, designed by Bristol but now manufactured by that company's rival, Rolls-Royce, after Bristol's take-over. Supersonic performance for any future Harrier derivative will be dependent on the greater thrust of a plenum-chamber burning engine, seen here in the form of the pioneering BS.100.
Right: The radical configuration of the Pegasus is well displayed by these engines under final assembly.
Below: Compared with the P.1127, the Kestrel and Harrier (here seen in the guise of a Harrier GR. Mk 1 of No. 4 Squadron) had a distinctly 'humped' look to the fuselage over the wing.

Left: The cockpit display of the Sea Harrier
Above: The cockpit equipment of the Sea Harrier is nicely grouped in ergonomic terms, with engine and electrical controls to the left and right of the seat, with weapon controls and flight information above the left and right rudder pedals, flanking the radar display unit.
Right: Pilot's eye view of the Harrier cockpit, showing older design.
Below: The complex but compact Blue Fox radar of the Sea Harrier.

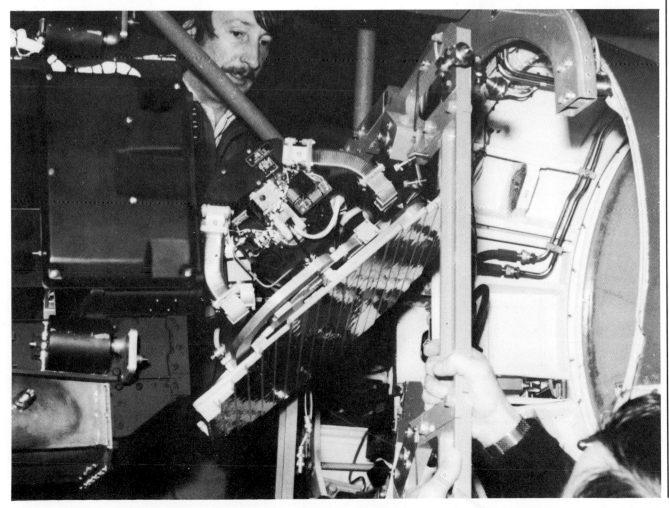

Hawker Kestrel

The decision to form the Tripartite Evaluation Squadron (TES, with air crew, and ground crew from Federal Germany, the UK and the USA) meant that more aircraft were needed. It was soon decided that though these need not be fully militarised aircraft with extensive weapon capability, it was in the interests of all concerned to produce an aircraft with greater capability, both military and in flight performance, than the basic P.1127. On 21 May 1962, therefore, the Ministry of Aviation ordered nine Hawker **Kestrel** aircraft (18 aircraft had at first been planned as the complement of the TES, but this figure was reduced to save capital expenditure). The key to the new aircraft, which was to be capable of operations in all visual flight rules (VFR) conditions with a nominal military load, was inevitably an improved and uprated engine, in this case designated the Pegasus 5. Bristol Siddeley Engines Ltd (formed by the amalgamation of Bristol Aero-Engines with Armstrong Siddeley Motors Ltd in April 1959) took the opportunity to recast the basic engine once again, principally by replacing the original fan type, based on the Olympus engine, with a completely new unit of three stages. No inlet guide vanes were fitted, but upstream of the high-pressure compressor the design incorporated a set of variable inlet guide vanes. The compressor itself was of advanced design with titanium blades, and the first-stage high-pressure turbine had air-cooled blades. The combustion chamber was also modified to become a fully annular type. First flown in February 1965, the Pegasus 5 was theoretically rated at 18,000-lb (8,165-kg) thrust, but to save development time and finance, was derated to 15,500-lb (7,031-kg) thrust for use in the Kestrel.

The aircraft itself was modelled closely on the P.1127, but reworked to take advantage of the lessons learned with the now extensive P.1127 flight programme. The main change was to the wing, which was entirely new and swept on both the leading and trailing edges, the former to a greater degree than either of the two planforms used in the P.1127. The wing was also of slightly less span than that of earlier aircraft, and the thicker wing root altered the appearance of the Kestrel, giving it a fairly pronounced hump behind the cockpit. Two stores pylons could be bolted under the wings. The fuselage was also altered, being lengthened in comparison with that of the P.1127 by the addition of extra bays on top of the forward nozzles and below the rear nozzles, this having the effect of shifting the wing slightly to the rear. A better relationship was established between the wing's centre of pressure, the aircraft's centre of gravity and the position of the nozzles by these changes, which were supplemented by the slight forward movement of the rear nozzles, made possible by the more acute bifurcation of the jetpipe. Another standard feature of the Kestrel, tested on the later P.1127s, was the use of a pair of ventral strakes to increase underfuselage pressure in low-altitude hovering by the trapping of gases. The instrument boom of the P.1127s was replaced by a camera installation on the Kestrels, and the door of the rear main landing gear unit was restressed to serve as an all-speed ventral airbrake.

The new aircraft was officially designated **Kestrel F(GA). Mk 1**, for Fighter (Ground-Attack) Mk 1,

The first Kestrel evaluation aircraft sports the unique markings of the Tripartite Evaluation Squadron.

XS691 was the fourth Kestrel, and first flew in September 1964. It was later sold to the USA, where it was redesignated XV-6A and given the serial 64-18265.

and the first of the nine examples flew on 7 March 1964. It was preceded by the last of the six P.1127s, which had been completed virtually to Kestrel standard. An intensive flight-test programme led to the clearance of the Kestrel for service operations in December 1964, the first time any VTO aircraft other than rotary-wing types had ever received such clearance.

With a complement of nine Kestrels and the last P.1127, the TES was formed at Dunsfold, the Hawker Siddeley main test field, on 15 October 1964, with Wing Commander D. McL. Scrimgeour as its commanding officer. This was the world's first VTOL fixed-wing squadron, and after initial working up at Dunsfold, the unit switched its base to RAF West Raynham in Norfolk. From this base the TES began operational evaluation of the Kestrel, with emphasis not so much on weapons aspects as the operational flexibility bestowed by the Kestrels' V/STOL capability for factors such as dispersed operations and maintenance, off-airfield logistics and other factors affecting the ability of the Kestrel to perform away from established facilities. The fixed evaluation programme lasted from April to November 1965, and in the course of this period the 10 aircraft flew some 600 hours in about 940 missions. The programme proved conclusively that the V/STOL fixed-wing aircraft could undertake a number of tasks all but impossible for aircraft of conventional take-off limitations, and the ability of the aircraft to perform reliably under adverse maintenance conditions impressed all involved, who included air and ground personnel from the RAF, Federal German Luftwaffe, the US Air Force, the US Navy and the US Army. Further trials were carried out up to April 1966, when six of the Kestrels were sold to the USA at knock-down prices for use in a variety of research roles unconnected directly with military developments. In US service the Kestrels were designated **XV-6A**, and made considerable contributions to V/STOL technology and capability in shipboard operations and the like.

Only two Kestrels remained in British hands (the last machine had been written off during the TES programme), and these were used for experimental programmes at the Blind Landing Experimental Unit at the RAF Bedford.

Supersonic waste: Hawker P.1154

An obsession with Mach 2 performance coloured much of the Western world's aircraft development programmes in the late 1950s and during the 1960s, this official predilection with outright performance helping to obscure the benefits of several otherwise useful programmes that might have borne useful fruit at relatively little cost. By the late 1950s NATO planning staffs were considering the uses of V/STOL aircraft with subsonic performance, but only a year or so later, in 1960, had plumped for truly supersonic performance, preferably in the Mach 2 class at medium and high altitude. It was an unfortunate decision, for while subsonic V/STOL aircraft were well within the current state of the art, supersonic aircraft of this category demanded considerably more research and development, both of which could only be devoted to newer projects at the expense of those already under way.

Nevertheless, both Bristol Siddeley and Hawker appreciated the way that matters were progressing, and during the late 1950s began to divert their attentions towards supersonic V/STOL. The key to such performance, as all parties readily agreed, was considerably enhanced powerplant performance. And here Hooker arrived at a neat solution: whereas conventional turbine engines could be boosted by burning extra fuel in the jetpipe (afterburning or reheat), Hooker rightly saw that in the vectored thrust engine the optimum volume for boost was the plenum chamber between the fan and the forward nozzles. Here air was compressed with its full ratio of oxygen, and the burning

of extra fuel would provide a very considerable increase of thrust. Such plenum-chamber burning was proposed for a modified Pegasus 5, with the promise of thrust raised from 15,500 lb (7,031 kg) to 20,500 lb (9,299 kg). Even more advanced was another Hooker proposal, this time for the BS.100, a vectored-thrust powerplant using much of the technology of the Olympus 22R engine developed for the abortive BAC TSR.2 aircraft, and fitted with plenum-chamber burning capability.

The Pegasus 5 development could be available in a considerably shorter time span, and Camm thus opted slightly unwillingly for this powerplant in the Hawker **P.1150** supersonic V/STOL design to meet the NBMR-3 specification. Finalised by Hooper, the P.1150 was essentially a refined version of the P.1127 with considerably more fuel, a longer fuselage of finer lines, a swept wing of reduced thickness/chord ratio, massive sharp-lipped inlets and a pair of stores pylons under each wing. A bold but practical design, the P.1150 could meet all the requirements of NBMR-3 (speed of Mach 1.5 at medium altitude) except a mission radius of 250 miles (402 km) with an underwing load of 2,000 lb (907 kg). But Bristol Siddeley was ready with yet another engine development, the Pegasus 6 rated at 19,000-lb (8,618-kg) thrust and offering the possibility of about 25,000-lb (11,340-kg) thrust with plenum-chamber burning. Hooper stretched the basic P.1150 design to accommodate the Pegasus 6, but was not satisfied and turned to other possibilities. The final Hawker proposal, one of

40 design contenders from 23 companies, was the potentially world-beating **P.1154** designed around the BS.100 derated to a thrust of 30,000 lb (13,608 kg) but still offering V/STOL performance, phenomenal acceleration and a maximum speed in the order of Mach 2.

Here the whole project nearly foundered on the twin rocks of NATO's existence as a command rather than procurement structure, with only an advisory capacity in members' actual procurement plans, and the obdurate opposition of Rolls-Royce to any V/STOL project that did not contain a battery of Rolls-Royce's lift engines. Thus while the NBMR-3 competition was won by the P.1154 design, the opposition of Rolls-Royce was sufficient for the Dassault Mirage IIIV to be appended as of equal capability as the P.1154. In the event neither of the designs was ordered as a NATO programme.

Oddly enough, the P.1154 did find favour in British corridors of power, for at last V/STOL had come out of the wilderness and started to become acceptable as a capability for service equipment. The fallacies of the 1957 White Paper were at last being seen for what they were, and with the failure of the NBMR-3 competition, it was appreciated in the UK that the P.1154 might prove an ideal replacement for the RAF's and Fleet Air Arm's obsolescent Hawker Hunter and de Havilland Sea Vixen fighters. In March 1962, therefore, the Ministry of Defence began the inevitably abortive process of trying to satisfy two conflicting requirements with a single design: the RAF wanted a low-level single-seat attack fighter, while the Royal Navy decided it needed a high-level two-seat air superiority fighter. Hawker began a complex series of modifications to produce the **P.1154RAF** and the **P.1154RN**, while a continuing spate of service demands meant that the two designs slowly lost all they had in common.

Delay after delay, combined with steady pressure from Rolls-Royce, which extolled the virtues of a Spey-powered version of the McDonnell F-4 Phantom as a cheaper, more capable and more quickly developed alternative to the P.1154RN, finally persuaded the Royal Navy to cancel the P.1154RN in February 1964. The RAF decided to press on with the P.1154RAF, and without the distractions of the naval pro-gramme rapid progress was made. The first prototype was in final assembly during October 1964, when the election of a Labour government spelled the end of this ambitious British project, cancelled in February 1965 on the grounds that the P.1154RAF could not be brought into service

before the Hunters it was to replace were grounded for struc-tural reasons. The speciousness of this argument is shown by the fact that the Spey-engined Phantoms ordered as a substitute did not begin to enter service until 1969, and by the fact that substantial numbers of Hunters are still in faithful service during the early 1980s.

The one good thing to emerge from the sorry tale of the P.1154 was the BS.100 engine. Though this did not enter service, the construction and testing of this advanced powerplant provided inestimable benefits in plenum-chamber burning technology. The first BS.100 ran in October 1964, and by December of the same year had been operated at thrust ratings in excess of 30,000 lb (13,608 kg) with plenum-chamber burning and without problems. The version of the

BS.100 selected for the P.1154RN was the BS.100/9 rated at 35,800-lb (16,239-kg) thrust, and there seems little doubt that this great engine could easily have been developed to this rating and higher. Rolls-Royce had assiduously fostered its lift-jet concept and, failing this, the notion of the Spey fitted for vectored thrust. The success of the BS.100 series was a major incentive for Rolls-Royce's pur-chase of Bristol Siddeley Engines Ltd in 1966, whereupon BSEL became the Bristol Engine Division of Rolls-Royce. Having backed the wrong V/STOL horse, this was the only way in which Rolls-Royce could maintain its position at the forefront of military powerplant technology.

The P.1154RAF would have given the RAF much enhanced operational capability in the 1970s, but was cancelled in 1965.

Hawker Siddeley P.1127 RAF

Though ultimately a waste of time and money, the saga of the P.1154 and its varied developments did show that there was at last a genuine British involvement in the eventual procurement of a V/STOL combat aircraft. This interest depended on the relationship of the Ministry of Defence with a Conservative administration. All this was ended with the arrival of Harold Wilson's Labour government in October 1964. Already antagonistic to the British aerospace industry for doctrinaire reasons, the Labour government's dissatisfaction was confirmed by the internecine struggle between Bristol Siddeley and Rolls-Royce, and worsened by the comparable antipathy between the RAF and Royal Navy. Thus it was only thanks to the sterling efforts of successive Chiefs of the Air Staff that the Labour government unwillingly permitted the limited development of the P.1127/Pegasus combination into the P.1127RAF by combining the previous combination (in refined form) with the navigation and attack system originally intended for the P.1154RAF.

All this behind-the-scenes manoeuvring had been taking place while the P.1154 was in its death throes, and it was only a fortnight after the cancellation of the P.1154 that Hawker Siddeley received a contract for six preproduction close-support and reconnaissance aircraft (XV276–XV281) designated P.1127RAF and finally named Harrier, which was to have been the service name of the P.1154. The essence of the new project was speed, and Hawker Siddeley were thus faced with the problem of combining a moderately refined Kestrel airframe with an uprated Pegasus engine and the electronics of the P.1154. The Kestrel

had proved itself a far superior aerodynamic vehicle to the P.1127, especially when tailplane span was increased by 2 ft (0.91 m) to 14 ft (4.27 m), but the designers appreciated fully that a more powerful engine would again lead to the type of longitudinal instability that had caused some tricky moments with the P.1127, and that an ordinary service aircraft would therefore require a good deal of redesigning. The problem facing the designers, therefore, was that of producing a service aircraft to be flown by normal squadron pilots, the starting point being the Kestrel, which was more suitable for pilots of well above average qualifications. The problem was both eased and exacerbated by the prospective use of the Pegasus 6 with about 25 per cent more power than the Pegasus 5.

What emerged in the P.1127RAF was thus a virtually new aircraft, with little more than the basic concept and many of the aerodynamic features of the P.1127 and the Kestrel. The problems to be overcome were legion, but the most important were a revised structure assured of a service life of 15,000 hours, even with the aircraft operating from dispersed locations; wholly new systems optimised for the off-base operations envisaged for the P.1127RAF, and so designed for minimum maintenance; alteration of the rear fuselage and tail unit to obviate the fatigue problem that had threatened the earlier designs' tails, which vibrated considerably when the engine was run up to high power settings on the ground with the nozzles trained aft; provision of markedly improved handling characteristics throughout a flight envelope that encompassed a unique speed

range of backward flight at up to 60 mph (97 km/h) and forward flight at up to Mach 1.25; improvement of longitudinal stability in all flight regimes with the wide range of external stores envisaged; and maintenance of the correct relationship of the centre of gravity with the centre of thrust for control in hovering flight.

The overall problem was somewhat eased by the rearward shift, in relative terms, of the engine in the Kestrel design. This could be retained for the P.1127RAF, which was officially named **Harrier** early in 1967, so that the designers (with John Fozard increasingly to the fore) were not faced with a complete reworking of the fuselage's basic dispositions. Thought was given to the enlargement of the wing to cater for greater operational weights, but current thinking was that a small wing was preferable for better high-speed cruise and for low gust response at high speeds and low levels. The definitive wing was a one-piece structure set in the shoulder position with an incidence of 1° 45' and anhedral of 12° on each panel. The wing was designed to the safe-life philosophy, and based on three aluminium alloy spars and integrally machined skins. Control and high-lift devices were also kept simple, and comprised plain ailerons and flaps of aluminium alloy honeycomb construction. Quarter-chord sweep was 34°, and the leading edge was fitted with a small dogtooth, effectively increasing outboard chord in conjunction with a curved streamwise tip outside the outrigger fairing, the latter to move the centre of lift marginally to the rear. Each wing was provided with two stores pylons, the inner unit cleared to 1,200 lb (544 kg) and the outer unit to 650 lb (295 kg).

The tail unit was of similar construction, with aluminium alloy honeycomb used for the unpowered rudder and the rear portion of the one-piece powered tailplane. This latter had undergone considerable evolution since the days of the first prototype P.1127, which had featured a flat tailplane spanning 12 ft (3.66 m). As noted above, the Kestrel had introduced a kinked 2 ft (0.91 m) increase in tailplane span, and an anhedral of 15°. The tailplane of the P.1127RAF was modelled aerodynamically on that of the Kestrel, but anhedral was increased to 18° and the structure was beefed-up at a weight increase initially of 24 lb (10.89 kg) and later of an extra 8 lb (3.63 kg) to provide the strength necessary to deal with the vibration factor associated with the turbulent efflux of the engine with the nozzles in the rearward-facing position.

The fuselage was a perfectly conventional structure of the semi-monocoque type, built to the safe-life principle on the basis of frames and stringers. The chief structural medium was aluminium alloy, though titanium was used near the tail and in areas by the nozzles where high temperatures might be expected. The power-plant was installed and maintained through the top of the fuselage, and the pilot was accommodated in a pressurised, heated and air-conditioned cockpit on a Martin-Baker Mk 9A or Mk 9D zero/zero ejector seat operating through the canopy shattered by means of a miniature detonating chord in an emergency. The landing gear configuration pioneered by the P.1127 was retained, but Dowty Rotol much refined the entire system to provide greater stability on the ground.

The chosen powerplant was the Pegasus 6, and much design effort went into the improvement of the inlets to make possible the optimum use of this engine's potentially greater thrust rating by dealing adequately with the greater airflow of this and later

engines. The solution adopted for the P.1127RAF was an enlarged pair of inlets with an uncomplicated variable-geometry system to tailor the airflow to operating conditions. The lips of the inlets were given the same type of leading edge as the wings, which delayed the onset of transonic drag rise but also minimised sideways spillage of the vital airflow, and control of this airflow was improved by the provision of a bleed door for the boundary layer in the side of the fuselage by the cockpit (already pioneered in the Kestrel) and the installation of six (later eight) auxiliary blow-in doors around the inlet cowl to reduce pressure loss in hovering flight. Clearly the perfect synchronisation of the four nozzles (two cold at the front and two hot at the rear) had been of paramount importance throughout the development history of the aircraft, and in the pre-production P.1127RAF batch great emphasis was placed on the reliability and redundancy of the synchronisation system, to ensure the perfectly concerted movement of all four nozzles when actuated by the simple lever beside the throttle in the cockpit.

Among the greatest efforts that went into the P.1127RAF were those concerned with the controls and the electronics. The reaction control valve system of the Kestrel was retained but with improvements, the intermittent type of control having proved its worth compared with the continuous bleed type by virtue of the reduced thrust loss at the nozzles (each 1 lb/0.45 kg per second mass flow through the reaction control valves reduced nozzle thrust by some 70 lb/ 31.8 kg). The reaction control valves (located at the front of the outrigger fairings for control in roll, at the front and rear of the fuselage for control in pitch, and at the rear of the fuselage for control in yaw) were not simple

units instructed merely to turn on or off, but divergent nozzles with swinging shutters operated by the adjacent conventional control surface, so that fine control was achieved by greater or lesser movement of the pilot's cockpit controls (control column and rudder pedals). The whole system proved highly effective, if a trifle on the sensitive side.

As mentioned above, the wings were each fitted for a pair of stores pylons. The rest of the P.1127RAF's offensive load was carried under the fuselage, which was provided with three hard-points: the centreline point was stressed to 1,200 lb (544 kg), and the outer points were designed to accommodate a pair of 30-mm Aden cannon pods with 130 rounds per gun. These pods were designed to act as pressure-trapping strakes to improve hovering performance, and were replaced by metal strakes when no gun armament was fitted. The nominal weapons load was thus 4,900 lb (2,223 kg) plus two Aden Mk 4 cannon pods, but by 1973 Harriers had been demonstrated with loads of more than 8,000 lb (3,629 kg). The inboard wing pylons and centreline fuselage hardpoint were eventually cleared for loads up to 2,000 lb (907 kg) each. The wing hardpoints are also plumbed for auxiliary tanks, either 330-Imp gal (1,500-litre) ferry tanks or 100-Imp gal (455-litre) jettisonable combat tanks, this extra capacity supplementing the internal 630 Imp gal (2,864 litres) carried in five fuselage and two wing tanks, all of them integral structures. Early in the P.1127RAF programme provision was made for inflight refuelling: a connection to the fuel tanks was run from a point on the upper side of the port inlet, and the required long angled inflight-refuelling probe could be attached to this point, the probe designed so that its tip was above and to the left of the pilot for good visibility during inflight-refuelling manoeuvres.

To complete the P.1127RAF's operational equipment electronic 'black boxes' were added wherever there was adequate volume within the airframe. (These are detailed in the technical specifications on page 54). In any event, many of the 'black boxes' were not fitted to the first P.1127RAF (XV276), which was flown by Bedford on 31 August 1966. Intensive flight and equipment trials were soon under way with this aircraft and its successors, and these trials gave ample proof of the P.1127RAF's potent capabilities as an operational platform.

Right: Boarding a two-seat Harrier. Easily seen in the open cockpit canopy are the lines of miniature detonating cord to shatter the plexiglass just before an ejected departure. Also visible is the undernose control valve for pitch control in the hover and transition.
Below: A Harrier GR. Mk 1 hovers above the helicopter pad of HMS *Blake*.

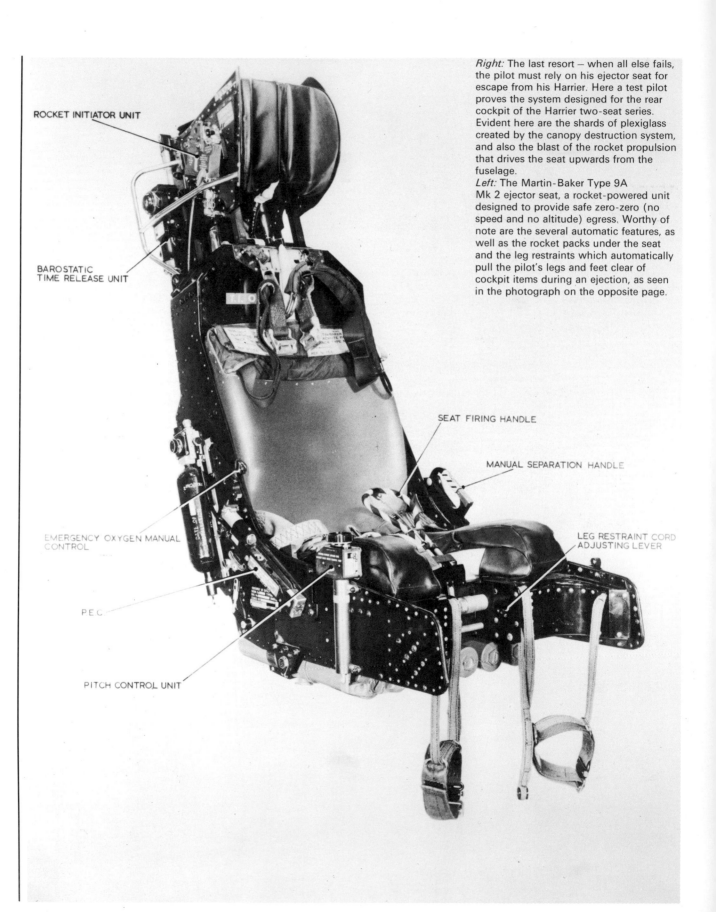

ROCKET INITIATOR UNIT

BAROSTATIC
TIME RELEASE UNIT

EMERGENCY OXYGEN MANUAL
CONTROL

P.E.C.

PITCH CONTROL UNIT

SEAT FIRING HANDLE

MANUAL SEPARATION HANDLE

LEG RESTRAINT CORD
ADJUSTING LEVER

Right: The last resort — when all else fails, the pilot must rely on his ejector seat for escape from his Harrier. Here a test pilot proves the system designed for the rear cockpit of the Harrier two-seat series. Evident here are the shards of plexiglass created by the canopy destruction system, and also the blast of the rocket propulsion that drives the seat upwards from the fuselage.

Left: The Martin-Baker Type 9A Mk 2 ejector seat, a rocket-powered unit designed to provide safe zero-zero (no speed and no altitude) egress. Worthy of note are the several automatic features, as well as the rocket packs under the seat and the leg restraints which automatically pull the pilot's legs and feet clear of cockpit items during an ejection, as seen in the photograph on the opposite page.

Hawker Siddeley Harrier GR. Mk 1

For political reasons the Labour government had seen fit to emphasise the P.1127RAF's research and development role, but it soon became clear that the RAF was soon to receive a new type of combat aircraft for which the P.1127RAF was merely a pre-production type. Thus Hawker Siddeley were informed, as the first P.1127RAF began its flight trials, that production contracts would soon be placed. Early in 1967 the company was contracted for the supply of 60 **Harrier GR. Mk 1** ground-attack and reconnaissance aircraft.

As production slowly gathered momentum, the P.1127RAF programme moved ahead without any major hitches, most of the concepts and hardware in the aircraft having been validated by the already protracted development history of the family. Emphasis had been placed, in the design of the P.1127RAF, on ease and reliability of control, particularly in the hover and transition phases of flight, and this aspect was refined by the test programme. The designers had made every endeavour to make the aircraft flyable in all flight regimes without an auto-stabilisation system, and though they were successful in this respect, the P.1127RAF was in fact fitted with a rudimentary autostabilisation system provided by Fairey and based on the system designed for the P.1154. Given the good manual hover and transition characteristics of the P.1127RAF, it was decided that a simple monoplex auto-stabilisation system would suffice, and though this was at first fitted as a low-authority control on the roll and pitch axes alone, it was later extended to take in the yaw axis.

Great effort went into the development of the Pegasus 6 engine in its Mk 101 form to improve control sensitivity and speed of response, both very significant in the safe use of the VTO and STO modes. Very useful results were obtained, and by the early 1970s the Pegasus Mk 101

A Harrier GR. Mk 1 of No. 3 Squadron lifts off with an underwing load made up of two rocket-launcher pods (outboard stations) and two drop tanks (inboard stations) as well as a pair of 30-mm Aden cannon packs under the fuselage.

could be opened up from half to full revolutions in a mere 2½ seconds. Hand in hand with these engine developments went further enhancement of the nozzle actuation mechanism to ensure that there was no delay or inaccuracy in the swivelling of the nozzles.

The installation and proving of the electronic systems was much more complicated, notably the inertial navigation and attack system designed to permit the pilot to fly at high speed and low level with an absolute certainty as to his position relative to potentially dangerous features in the terrain, and to known enemy dispositions. Only in such a way could the pilot hope to achieve satisfactory attack results with the blind first-pass engagement necessary to provide a reasonable chance of escape.

All six P.1127RAF aircraft had been delivered by August 1967, and production of the first service model, the Harrier GR. Mk 1, was well under way, the first such aircraft (XV738) being flown by Duncan Simpson on 28 December 1967. During 1968 this and subsequent production Harrier GR. Mk 1s were used primarily for the development of operational-standard electronics and the evolution of a flying syllabus for an aircraft which, on entry into regular RAF service, would be as radical as any aircraft yet received by the service.

The first RAF unit to receive the Harrier GR. Mk 1 was the Harrier Conversion Unit, which was formed at Dunsfold in January 1969. The choice of a company airfield was made to facilitate liaison with the manufacturer, and the decision proved invaluable in ironing out the problems that inevitably crept into the programme as pilots new to the aircraft became slowly familiar with their new mounts. On 1 April 1969, the 51st birthday of the RAF, the Harrier GR. Mk 1 officially entered service when the Harrier Conversion Unit became No. 233 Operational Conversion Unit and shifted its base to RAF Wittering in Northamptonshire. Rapid progress had been made in devising a conversion programme, and in July 1969 No. 1 Squadron moved to Wittering to start its conversion from Hunters to the Harrier. The next three units to receive the Harrier were Nos 4, 20 and 3 Squadrons, which after conversion moved to RAF Wildenrath in Federal Germany to become the first operational V/STOL wing on 1 January 1972.

Meanwhile, further improvements had been made to the Pegasus engine, the Pegasus 10 being rated at 20,500-lb (9,299-kg) thrust before it entered service with the RAF as the Pegasus Mk 102. There was little that was completely new in the engine, but better cooling of the high-pressure turbine blades and the combustion chambers, plus improved water-injection and fuel pump systems added the extra thrust while also improving reliability. Harrier GR. Mk 1s retro-fitted with the Pegasus Mk 102 were redesignated Harrier GR. Mk 1As. Another benefit for the Harrier force during 1969 was an optional ferry wingtip of increased span. This could be bolted onto any aircraft, the greater span increasing the aspect ratio of the wing and so reducing induced drag with a consequent increase in the range attainable with a given quantity of fuel.

No. 20 Squadron did not long survive as a Harrier unit, for in 1977 it converted to SEPECAT Jaguar strike aircraft, the squadron's aircraft being distributed to Nos 3 and 4 squadrons to raise their establishment to the NATO norm of 18 aircraft per squadron.

The primary task of the Harrier squadrons during their first years of service with the type was a full examination of operational requirements and capabilities, ranging from the survey of enormous numbers of possible dispersed sites for wartime operations, to the nature and variety of ground-attack roles that could be undertaken with the increasingly diverse weapon load being approved for service deployment. It was rapidly appreciated that while the Harriers could be deployed to very remote, even agricultural or forest sites, their capabilities were enhanced by the ready availability of a fairly sizable quantity of support equipment (all brought

in by road from main operating bases), and of a stretch of level ground, preferably about 450 yards (410 m) long, to allow the Harriers to take-off after a short run rather than vertically. Even a short run proved adequate to give the Harrier greater operational capability, for the quantity of wing lift generated in this run allowed the aircraft to carry a greater load of weapons and/or fuel. The technique evolved for such STO operations was to set the nozzle control lever stop at the 60° position, but then pull the lever back to set the nozzles themselves in the horizontal position for maximum acceler-

ation of the aircraft along the ground; then at the critical moment the lever was slammed against the stop, the swift rotation of the nozzles from the horizontal to the angled position ensuring that the aircraft bounded into the sky, where the nozzles could again be turned to the rear to build up true flying speed.

At the end of a mission either a vertical landing or a rolling vertical landing was the optimum manoeuvre, the latter being better suited to operations at dispersed sites as it prevented the ingestion of loose material thrown up by the downward blast of the engine.

Left: A Land Rover tows the Harrier GR. Mk 1 of Flight Lieutenant L. S. Penny (No. 1 Squadron) from its camouflaged dispersal point during field exercises in 1971. For optimum use of the Harrier, the bay would normally have had a pierced-steel planking or MEXE strip to avoid surface erosion and problems with mud. *Below:* RAF armourers work on the 19-tube port SNEB rocket launcher of this Harrier GR. Mk 1 of No. 233 Operational Conversion Unit. Note the depth of the Aden cannon pods under the fuselage, designed to trap high-pressure gases and improve hover.

Hawker Siddeley Harrier T. Mk 2

The Spanish navy has two VAE-1 Matador two-seaters on the strength of its sole V/STOL unit, Escuadrilla 008. This is aircraft no. 8, procured as a TAV-8S.

Given the radical nature of the Harrier, it would have been only sensible for the type to have been produced first as a two-seat conversion trainer, or at least for the trainer to have been produced at the same time as the single-seat operational version. But this was not to be, largely for lack of finance. The first Hawker proposal for such an aircraft was formed in September 1960, and would have provided a two-seat P.1127 aircraft. But nothing was done, and it was 1965 before Hawker Siddeley again turned their minds to such a type, in 1965 conducting a feasibility study into the possibility of a two-seat version of the P.1127RAF. However, it was not until 1970 was well advanced that Hawker Siddeley received a contract for two prototype two-seaters, which were allocated the serials XW174 and XW175 These were only development aircraft, and the first made its maiden flight on 24 April 1969.

Meanwhile Hawker Siddeley had been contracted to develop a two-seat conversion trainer which was also to be used for proficiency training in the single-seater's navigation and attack system, a function which could have been performed just as well by an existing two-seat trainer (the Hunter T. Mk 7, for example) modified with the necessary electronic gear. But the Air Staff's primary reasoning in demanding a dual-role two-seater was the RAF's need to have the **Harrier T. Mk 2**, as the type was designated, as a supplement to the single-seaters for combat use in emergencies.

To provide the extra cockpit volume for the second seat and its associated controls and instrument panels, the forward fuselage had to be lengthened by some 3 ft 11 in (1.19 m), while the seat frame of the single-seater, which now became the seat frame of the instructor in the rear cockpit, was relocated 7 in

(0.178 m) farther aft. At the same time the nose-mounted reaction control valve was shifted forward almost to the very nose, and a number of cockpit associated systems were repackaged in altered locations. The inertial platform and the camera had to be found new homes, and were placed under the rear seat, which was raised above the level of the forward seat to give the instructor adequate vision ahead and downwards. Oddly enough, the elevation of the rear seat was achieved without drag penalty, and the instructor enjoyed a better field of vision than the single-seat pilot.

The extra forward area would have destabilised the aircraft, and to prevent this the tail unit was lengthened by 33.33 in (0.847 m). At the same time the empennage was raised by 11 in (0.279 m) by relocation to a platform built up from the existing rear fuselage structure. The tailcone was also increased appreciably in length to shift the rear reaction control valve farther aft and to provide, at least during the development phase of the Harrier T. Mk 2's career, a housing for the anti-spin parachute. Test flying revealed that further modifications were necessary to maintain directional stability at high angles of attack, and the fin was ultimately increased in height by 1 ft 6 in (0.457 m) and made broader in chord. The evolution of this revised vertical tail proceeded in parallel with production of the Harrier T. Mk 2, and the larger vertical tail was retrofitted as soon as possible to in-service Harrier trainers. The first Harrier T. Mk 2 was XW264, and made its maiden flight on 24 April 1969.

Like the Harrier GR. Mk 1, the Harrier T. Mk 2 was retrofitted with the Pegasus Mk 102 when it was available, re-engined aircraft being redesignated Harrier T. Mk 2As.

Hawker Siddeley Harrier GR. Mk 3 and Harrier T. Mk 4

Engine development had been matching airframe progress closely, and in February 1971 the new Pegasus 11 was exhaustively tested, receiving service clearance in July 1971 as the Pegasus Mk 103. The Pegasus Mk 103 benefited from a fan stage with new blades to increase the mass of air that could be handled, and this was combined with improved cooling of the high-pressure turbine to allow higher combustion temperatures. Some nice calculations were necessary to balance the hot-gas output from the rear nozzles and the cold-gas output from the front nozzles, but these were accomplished successfully, and the Pegasus Mk 103 is the standard engine used in Harriers during the early part of the 1980s. Existing Harriers were re-engined

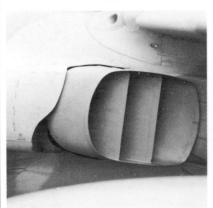 

Top left: The thimble nose of the Harrier GR. Mk 3 houses (rear) an F95 reconnaissance camera and (front) a Ferranti Type 106 laser ranger and marked-target seeker.

Top right: Equally important are the twin passive units of the Marconi Space and Defence Systems ARI.18223 radar warning receiver system, mounted on the fin and on the tailcone.

Centre left: Rear view of a Harrier GR. Mk 3 with external power connected.

Centre right: The Harrier GR. Mk 3 has eight suction-relief doors in each inlet.

Left: Each of the four nozzles is a two-vane cascade type, rotatable through 98°.

Right: Harrier GR. Mk 3 of No. 4 Squadron.

with the designations **Harrier GR. Mk 3** and **Harrier T. Mk 4**. As new-build Harrier GR. Mk 3s began to enter service in 1976, they were fitted with a Ferranti LRMTS (laser ranger and marked-target seeker) in a modified nose that altered the contours of the Harrier's appearance. Essentially the same unit as that fitted in the Jaguar, the LRMTS in the Harrier is used often for the acquisition of targets marked by the lasers of friendly ground forces, permitting the first-pass use of missiles using semi-active laser guidance, but more generally used to acquire a designated target whose range and position are then presented on the pilot's head-up display (HUD). In-service aircraft were already being retrofitted with the LRMTS when the first aircraft of the last Harrier GR. Mk 3 production

batch, provided with the LRMTS on the line, was delivered. By 1979 the RAF's entire Harrier force had been provided with the LRMTS nose, with consequent improvements in the accuracy of weapon delivery.

Another combat accessory of the period was a radar warning receiver (RWR), with two passive antennae on the tail: one located towards the top of the fin and covering the forward hemisphere; and the other perched at the extreme tip of the tail cone to cover the rearward hemisphere. This Marconi system, retrofitted to all in-service Harriers and built into new aircraft, provides the pilot with a warning whenever the aircraft is illuminated by radar, and also provides him with information as to the source's bearing and, in some circumstances, its type. The RWR is an invaluable combat tool.

Below: A trio of No. 3 Squadron Harrier GR. Mk 3s over Germany. Note the cooling air ram intake at the base of the fin.
Above right: Tandem cockpits and LRMTS nose of a Harrier T. Mk 4 trainer.
Right: Protective 'eyelids' over the port for the Ferranti Type 106 LRMTS.
Right below: A combat-capable Harrier T. Mk 4 (without LRMTS) of No. 233 OCU based at Wittering in Cambridgeshire.

Top: Revised upper fuselage of the Harrier T. Mk 4 with higher cockpit line.
Above: Port nozzles of the Pegasus Mk 103 used in the Harrier T. Mk 4.
Above right: Compared with the single-seaters, the Harrier trainer has a much revised tail, with larger vertical surfaces and an extended tailcone.
Right: The Dowty Rotol outrigger legs have 13.50 × 6.4 Dunlop wheels and tyres.

Hawker Siddeley/McDonnell Douglas AV-8A and TAV-8A

A V/STOL attack aircraft is ideally suited to the basic mission entrusted to the US Marine Corps, which must be ready to land from the sea and secure a beach-head anywhere in the world, supported by its own aircraft operating from carriers and improvised shore bases. Despite this, there was no US Marine Corps representation in the Tripartite Evaluation Squadron, though USMC professionals had long evinced an interest in the P.1127/Kestrel series as a potential purchase for Marine Air Wings. USMC pilots were able to fly the Kestrels bought by the USA as XV-6As, but found it difficult to persuade the Pentagon that a combat aircraft evolved from the XV-6A would be ideally suited to USMC

specific requirements. At the same time there was intense political and industrial pressure brought to bear against this non-American project (which had been largely financed by American money), and at times it looked impossible that the USMC might secure the aircraft it needed. In 1968 USMC pilots were able to test-fly the Harrier, and persuaded the American authorities after this that the type had the combat potential and range necessary for the USMC role. Finally permission was received for the purchase of enough aircraft to equip four operational squadrons, with a reserve for training and attrition replacement. Thus the total purchase was fixed at 114 aircraft, to be designated **AV-8A** in

American service. The AV-8A was very similar to the Harrier GR. Mk 1, but was intended from the start to have the Pegasus Mk 103, though 10 of the first 12 aircraft ordered from Hawker Siddeley were fitted at first with Pegasus Mk 102 powerplants. What was delivered to the US Marines, therefore was essentially a version of the Harrier GR. Mk 3, designated Harrier Mk 50 by Hawker Siddeley.

The first 12 AV-8As were ordered in 1969, and eventually the number bought from Hawker Siddeley totalled 110 aircraft: 102 AV-8A single-seaters and eight **TAV-8A** (Harrier Mk 54) two-seaters. Intended for fair-weather attack and air-combat, the AV-8As have less sophisticated navigation and attack systems than the British Harriers, but are equipped to carry a pair of AIM-9 Sidewinder air-to-air missiles in the air-combat role. In this latter capacity the pilots of the US Marine Corps have

Left: An AV-8A of VMA-231 (US Marine Corps Attack Squadron 231) in flight. Basically similar to the Harrier in airframe and powerplant, the AV-8A is optimised for a slightly different role, that of attack in the face of less sophisticated defences. The AV-8A is also a capable air-combat aircraft with AIM-9 Sidewinder missiles, cannon and VIFFing.
Below: VA-1 Matador of Escuadrilla 008. Note the forward pair of UHF blade aerials, the wide-blade VHF blade for communication with helicopters, and the rear tactical VHF blade aerial.
Right: One of the Spanish navy's two VAE-1 two-seat conversion trainers and, in the foreground, a Pegasus Mk 103 vectored-thrust turbofan.

developed a technique that gives the Harrier/AV-8A series a unique advantage in air combat. This technique is VIFFing (vectoring in forward flight), and was developed from active deceleration tests undertaken by Major Harry Blot, USMC, during 1971. Blot discovered that the vectoring of the nozzles while the aircraft was in wing-borne flight offered the possibility of applying upward or even rearward forces so concisely and powerfully that it would be impossible for even a dedicated air-combat pilot to stay on the tail of an alert Harrier/AV-8A pilot. Blot's initial feelings were confirmed in a series of test flights against agile aircraft, and VIFFing is now part of the combat repertoire of Harrier/AV-8A pilots.

The first AV-8A was handed over to the US Marine Corps on 20 November 1970, and the type was cleared for service deployment in March 1971. The first AV-8A squadron to form was VMA-513 at Beaufort, South

Carolina, in April 1971, and since that time the other USMC squadrons to operate the type have been VMA-542 and VMA-231, (together with VMA-513 the combat element of Marine Air Group 32), and the training squadron VMAT-203. The squadrons have confirmed fully the high expectations of the type in the late 1960s, operating from a variety of bases and also the USMC amphibious assault ships.

So far there has been one other customer for the AV-8A, the Spanish Navy, which in 1975 ordered six **AV-8S** single-seaters and two **TAV-8S** two-seaters for operations from the Spanish aircraft-carrier *Dédalo*. These aircraft were given American designations as they were bought by the Americans as kits for assembly by McDonnell Douglas before resale to the Spanish. This tortuous arrangement was designed to ensure that a Labour administration in the UK could not cancel the order. The Hawker

Siddeley and Spanish Navy designations for the two types were **Harrier Mk 55** and **VA-1 Matador** for the AV-8S, and **Harrier Mk 56** and **VAE-1 Matador** for the TAV-8S. A further five AV-8S aircraft were ordered in 1977, and the aircraft form the equipment of Escuadrilla 008, based at Rota but frequently operated from the *Dédalo* and slated for deployment to the new Spanish aircraft-carrier *Principe de Asturias*.

Survivors of the original AV-8A force are in the middle 1980s being upgraded to **AV-8C** standard with a host of avionics and systems improvements, many of them derived from the research undertaken to produce the McDonnell Douglas **AV-8B**. This upgrading will permit the original British-built batch to remain competitive in American terms while the USMC V/STOL force is augmented by the much improved AV-8B version, essentially an American-developed version.

British Aerospace Sea Harrier FRS. Mk 1

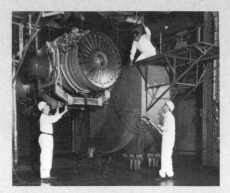

In 1963 Hawker Aircraft had become the Hawker-Blackburn Division of Hawker Siddeley Aviation; then in 1965 the company was reorganised as a single entity without divisions. This structure remained unaltered for 12 years, until Hawker Siddeley Aviation became a component of British Aerospace as the corporation's Kingston-Brough Division in 1977.

Hawker Siddeley had for some years discussed with its American licensee, McDonnell Douglas of St Louis, Missouri, the possibility of a joint undertaking to produce a Harrier optimised for naval use. The Harrier and its predecessors had undertaken frequent and highly successful trials and demonstrations aboard the aircraft-carriers of many navies in

the previous 15 years, and prospects seemed bright for a naval V/STOL aircraft, which offered the possibility of reducing the length of flight deck needed at a time when the cost of modern aircraft-carriers was becoming prohibitive not only to conventionally rich nations but also to the USA, that arch-proponent of naval air power.

But by 1975 the British government had decided that there was insufficient compatibility between Royal Navy and US Marine Corps requirements to produce a viable combat aircraft, and so instructed Hawker Siddeley to proceed with a purely British carrier-borne V/STOL aircraft. This emerged as the British Aerospace **Sea Harrier FRS. Mk 1**, designed for operations as a

fighter, reconnaissance and strike aircraft. The designers were able to make fairly rapid progress with the design, for the basic airframe and powerplant combination was already in existence, and the Royal Navy had as early as 1971 been considering with interest a Maritime Support Harrier, later known as the Maritime Harrier, which helped to finalise the operation features and electronics of the eventual Sea Harrier. However, a production decision was slower to materialise, and it was this that was announced in 1975. Progress with components was more decisively organised, for it was in 1973 that Rolls-Royce was instructed to move ahead with development of the navalised Pegasus 104 engine, and Ferranti received a contract for the proto-

Left: Test crew manoeuvre a Pegasus Mk 103 into its test cell. The Mk 104 of the Sea Harrier FRS. Mk 1 is only slightly different from the Mk 103, the chief modifications being the construction of the low-pressure and intermediate casings of corrosion-resistant materials and the strengthening of the gearbox drive to allow for greater electric power generation.
Right: A Sea Harrier FRS. Mk 1 of No. 800 Squadron, Fleet Air Arm.
Below: A Sea Harrier FRS. Mk 1 in low-visibility grey finish during 1982.

type construction of the necessary Blue Fox radar. The Pegasus Mk 104 is based on the Mk 103 engine with a number of purely naval ancillary equipment features, as well as changes in material to suit the engine for maritime operations: the casing for the fan is made of aluminium alloy instead of a magnesium/zirconium alloy, for example, to obviate the corrosion problems that would have beset a magnesium alloy in proximity with salt water; and sacrificial anodes are also built into the engine, which has a higher-capacity gearbox.

The task of Ferranti in developing the Blue Fox radar was eased by previous developments, in this case the Sea Spray radar already under development for the West-

land Lynx helicopter. The provision of radar was perhaps the single most important difference between the Harrier and Sea Harrier aircraft. Radar had frequently been discussed as a feature of the land-based Harrier, but had been decided against as not really essential to the Harrier's primary role, and also as leading to greatly increased costs. The Sea Harrier had radically different requirements, and for these a compact multi-mode radar was considered vital. Ferranti thus developed the excellent Blue Fox system, which weighs only 186 lb (84 kg) and offers the pilot a choice of four modes suiting the Sea Harrier to the air interception, plus the air-to-surface vessel search and strike role. The four operating

modes fixed for the Blue Fox system were thus search (with plan position indication or sector scan capability), attack (with lead-pursuit capability in the air attack role and weapon-aiming capability by means of the HUD in the surface attack role), bore-sight (for use in the event of chance encounters) and transponder (for the identification of IFF returns). In all, the Blue Fox radar is an impressive piece of equipment, with good range and reliability much better than that required or even anticipated. The whole package fits into a revised nose which hinges to port, so reducing overall length for carrier accommodation reasons.

The decision to use the Sea Harrier in the fighter as well as attack roles dictated an alteration in the cockpit configuration and position, for the Harrier had been finalised as a pure attack machine with little requirement for the 360° fields of vision required in a fighter. In the Sea Harrier, therefore, the whole cockpit section was raised by 11 in (0.279 m) to allow the installation of a bulged all-round vision canopy, which also offered considerably better fields of vision downwards. This alteration, which produced no adverse drag effects, also offered greater volume under the cockpit floor for the installation of equipment. Apart from the cockpit, radar and a number of electronic systems, the Sea Harrier is very similar to the basic Harrier GR. Mk 3, and can carry the same weapons load, although the type also has the facility to carry a pair of Sidewinder missiles for the air-to-air role, or a pair of air-to-surface missiles such as Sea Eagle or Harpoon for the air-to-surface role.

Initial production was fixed at 24 aircraft, principally for use on board the Royal Navy's new class of three small carriers, destined to enter service from the late 1970s. There were no prototypes, though the first three Sea Harrier FRS. Mk 1 aircraft (XZ438–XZ440) were used for trials with a mass of extra instrumentation. Various delays beset the production programme, and it was not until 20 August 1978 that the third Sea Harrier became the first of the marque to fly, some 13 months later than planned. During 1978 another 10 Sea Harrier FRS. Mk 1s were ordered, and by early 1982 most of these had been delivered.

Early success with trials confirmed the considerably enhanced capabilities of the Sea Harrier in comparison with the Harrier, and interest in export purchases came from several countries. By 1982 the only interest turned into firm orders is that of India, which has contracted for six

Sea Harrier FRS. Mk 51 aircraft all but identical with the Royal Navy's Sea Harrier FRS. Mk 1, plus a pair of Sea Harrier T. Mk 60 dual-control trainers which will be navalised versions of the Harrier T. Mk 4.

Mention must also be made of a feature which had much improved the capability of Sea Harriers from small ships. This is the so-called 'ski-jump' devised by Lieutenant Commander Douglas Taylor, RN. This is a beautifully simple yet effective notion: an upward-curved ramp is built onto the bows of any ship designed for Sea Harrier operations, so that at the end of a roll horizontal take-off run, the aircraft is thrown into the air with

Below: A Sea Harrier FRS. Mk 1 (allocated to HMS *Invincible*) at the hover during a training flight.
Bottom: A Sea Harrier FRS. Mk 1 of No. 800 Squadron (based at RNAS Yeovilton but destined for HMS *Hermes*) shadows the beautiful Russian carrier *Kiev* on passage through the English Channel. Towards the rear of *Kiev*'s flightdeck are two examples of the world's only other operational VTOL aircraft, the Yakovlev Yak-36 'Forger', a far less capable combat aircraft.
Right: Pictured in a steep climb, a Harrier FRS. Mk 1 of No. 800 Squadron shows off its revised lines and armament, including a pair of Sidewinder AAMs.
Right, centre left: The Sea Harrier FRS. Mk 1 can carry up to 8,000 lb (3,629 kg) of assorted weapons, including such relatively unsophisticated devices as this pair of 'iron' bombs.
Right, centre right: Ski-jump take-off.
Bottom right: Sea Harrier FRS. Mk 1s of No. 800 Squadron during trials with HMS *Invincible*.

a useful vertical component that supplements wing lift and permits the carriage of more fuel and/or weapons than is possible with a conventional VTOL or even STOL take-off. Various ramp angles were tried, and it was finally established that an angle of 12° produced optimum results. Such ramps are now commonplace with vessels intended to deploy Sea Harriers and AV-8s, and have also proved useful on the occasions when land-based Harrier aircraft have been operated from ships.

Such an occasion was the Falklands War undertaken by the UK in May and June 1982 to recover possession of the Falkland Islands from an occupying Argentinian force. Some 28 Sea Harrier aircraft were deployed to the theatre in time for action, most of them aboard carriers of the South Atlantic Task Force, and it was the Sea Harriers that finally gave the family its first taste of combat more than 20 years after the first of the series began its flight trials. In the Falkland operations the Sea Harriers provided air cover for the task force as it approached the islands, and then fought off a number of determined Argentinian air attacks. When the British landing had been launched the Harriers were able to undertake their designated task of close air support, at first from ships of the task force but later from primitive land bases, while the Sea Harriers continued to provide air cover and to supplement the Harriers wherever possible. A number of Argentinian aircraft succumbed to the guns and missiles of the Sea Harriers, but the British also lost six Sea Harrier FRS. Mk 1 and four Harrier GR. Mk 3 aircraft, five of them to ground fire (either missiles or gunfire, in proportions yet to be determined accurately) and the other five in accidents. Further purchases of Sea Harriers and Harriers have been announced to make up combat and attrition losses.

McDonnell Douglas AV-8B and British Aerospace Harrier GR. Mk 5

There have been many proposals for advanced developments of the basic Harrier concept, but for financial reasons these have tended to come from the USA. This was made possible by the fact that in 1971 Hawker Siddeley and Rolls-Royce each signed licence-production agreements with American companies to ease the path towards an American purchase of the Harrier. Both British companies appreciated that the American administration would demand the right for licence production in the event of contracts for more than the original AV-8A and TAV-8A force, so Hawker Siddeley signed with McDonnell Douglas for the production and development in the airframe department, while Rolls-Royce signed a similar deal with Pratt & Whitney for the Pegasus engine, designated F402 in American service.

By the time these deals had been struck, Hawker Siddeley had already investigated a number of ideas for a 'Super Harrier' under the basic project designations **P.1184** and **P.1185**. These were all posited on the development of a Pegasus engine developing a thrust of about 25,000 lb (11,340 kg), a wholly reasonable assumption given the fact that a Pegasus 15 demonstrator had been run at 24,900-lb (11,295-kg) thrust during 1972. And this demonstrator was merely the fan of the proposed Pegasus 15, which had a diameter 2.25 in (5.715 cm) greater than that of earlier engines, added to the core of a standard Pegasus.

With American interest in the project assured by the Hawker Siddeley/McDonnell Douglas and Rolls-Royce/Pratt & Whitney deals, intergovernment and inter-company bodies were established to try to work out a viable common advanced version for co-production by the two countries. Various **Advanced Harrier** and **AV-16A** ideas were promoted, but all foundered for lack of interest, lack of finance, and politico-industrial opposition of one form or another. Over the years these projects centred on several key features of the basic V/STOL design: the cockpit, which was to be raised for better fields of vision; the wing, which was to be of greater area and revised aerofoil for better manoeuvrability and weapon load combined with greater range; the inlets, which were to be improved for increased airflow recovery and better cruise efficiency; the lift improvement devices, where the use of improved ventral strakes would materially increase maximum VTO weight; and the structure, where the use of composite materials would provide greater strength at reduced weight. At the same time the whole electronic suite of the proposed aircraft was to be modernised and upgraded in capability.

In 1975 the British government decided to call a halt to the joint proposals with the Americans on the grounds that insufficient common ground existed to make the Advanced Harrier AV-16A a viable proposition. From this time onwards British efforts were directed primarily towards an improved version of the basic Harrier, largely by the fitting of a

wing of better aerofoil and greater area to raise cruising performance, agility and payload, and by provision of leading-edge root extensions (LERXs) as a further aid to manoeuvrability. This 'Big-Wing' Harrier was regarded favourably by the RAF, either in the form of new-build aircraft or as a retrofit on existing aircraft, but by the late 1970s the British government had begun to move towards rejection of the proposal, mainly on grounds of economy.

The McDonnell Douglas AV-8B is a much improved aircraft compared with the AV-8A, and is here seen in the form of a development aircraft produced by conversion of an AV-8A airframe. The fuselage is largely unaltered, but has larger ventral strakes for greater pressure trapping, the effect of these being supplemented by a retractable flap aft of the noseleg. The wing is completely new, however, and is an exceptionally strong composite structure with less sweep but more area and span. Maximum weapon load in the VTO mode is 7,000 lb (3,175 kg) rising to 17,000 lb (7,711 kg) in the STO mode, the stores comprising two underfuselage gun pods, an underfuselage hardpoint and six underwing hardpoints. With the dismal refusal of the UK to participate fully in the AV-8B programme, world leadership in V/STOL combat technology has inevitably crossed the Atlantic to the USA.

McDonnell Douglas was already in the driving seat so far as major advances of the basic Harrier design philosophy were concerned. The company evolved from its so-called **AV-8A Plus** proposal a more definitive aircraft, originally tested in the form of two **YAV-8B** development machines modified from AV-8A aircraft. Flight tests confirmed the overall superiority of the YAV-8Bs over the standard AV-8A, and plans were finalised for the production-standard AV-8B, which resembles the original Harrier in overall configuration and concept, but is markedly different in most details. The cockpit is raised, in the same fashion as that of the Sea Harrier; the entirely new supercritical-section wing has greater span and area, and is based on a graphite epoxy composite main wing box and eight spars, the use of the box as an integral tank increasing fuel capacity by some 50 per cent in comparison with the Harrier; much improved ventral strakes have been added; the horizontal tail has a high proportion of composites in the structure; the rear of the fuselage had been lengthened by 1 ft 6 in (0.457 m); and the vertical tail has been enlarged in the fashion also adopted for the Sea Harrier. These are the obvious alterations, but a closer examination reveals other aspects such as altered flaps, modifications to the inlets

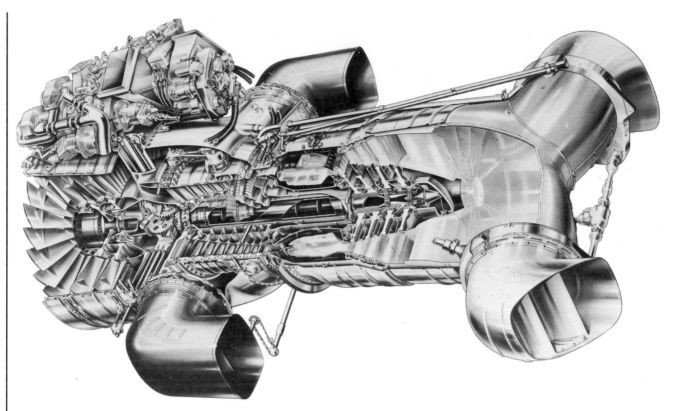

and a wide assortment of internal alterations. Also in the fashion that characterises US aircraft design, the various components that make up the entire system have been integrated in a way not really achieved with the Harrier, so that the AV-8B promises to be a more balanced combat aircraft.

In July 1981 the British recognised the virtues of the **AV-8B Harrier II**, and decided to order a batch of 60 to be designated **Harrier GR. Mk 5** in RAF service. These will be assembled in the UK, and a complex system of work-sharing has been organised between the airframe and engine partners on each side of the Atlantic, so that at least some of the financial return on this exciting new aircraft will come home to the basic design's country of origin. There exists in the USA a strong lobby opposed to USMC procurement of the proposed 336 AV-8Bs, but there seems every likelihood that the USMC's excellent record with the AV-8A will militate against the

abandonment of the project.

At the same time a number of yet more advanced projects (**AV-8E** improved AV-8B with uprated engine and LERXs, and **AV-8SX** supersonic demonstrator with PCB Pegasus 11F-35) have been schemed, but these are still very much at the paper stage, and if any of them materialise, it will surely be under the McDonnell Douglas aegis, even if British Aerospace is involved as a minor partner. The situation with the Pegasus engine is more promising for the UK, with a larger proportion of the development of plenum-chamber burning models being undertaken by Rolls-Royce.

The Harrier is now a well established series of aircraft, nearly 25 years old in terms of hardware, but the type had to overcome severe technical, financial and political opposition before its many virtues were fully appreciated. The Harrier series is still the world's only true V/STOL combat aircraft, and must still have a useful role to play in the years to come.

The engine for the AV-8B is designated F402-RR-406 by the Americans, and is basically similar to the Pegasus Mk 104 of the Sea Harrier FRS. Mk 1 apart from improvements to increase lift and mean time between overhauls. It also has greater electrical output.
Above: F402-RR-406 vectored-thrust turbofan. Note the mechanical linkages to ensure the symmetrical operation of the nozzles.

The Harrier in the Falklands Campaign

During the Falklands Campaign of April–June 1982, 28 Sea Harrier FRS. Mk 1 aircraft of the Fleet Air Arm and 14 Harrier GR. Mk 3 aircraft of the RAF were deployed to the South Atlantic, four of the Harriers arriving too late to see action. The Sea Harrier force flew more than 1,100 combat air patrols and 90 close support missions, losing six of their number (two of them to Argentine ground fire). On the credit side the Sea Harriers shot down at least 20 Argentinian aircraft (16 with Sidewinder AAMs and four with 30-mm cannon fire), and probably destroyed another three aircraft. The Harrier force flew some 125 close-support and tactical reconnaissance missions, losing four of their number (three of them to Argentinian ground fire).

British Aerospace Harrier GR. Mk 3 technical description

Wings: cantilever shoulder-wing monoplane structure with a Hawker Siddeley aerofoil section; quarter-chord sweep 34°; anhedral 12°; incidence 1° 45'; thickness/chord ratio decreasing from 10 per cent at the root to 5 per cent at the tip; the wing is a single safe-life structure of aluminium alloy, based on three spars with integrally machined skins and attached to the fuselage at six points; aluminium-alloy bonded honeycomb plain ailerons and flaps; reaction-control valve built into the front of each outrigger leg fairing; optional ferry tips can be bolted on in place of the normal tips, the ferry tips increasing aspect ratio and thus reducing induced drag; extra span conferred by ferry tips is 4 ft 5 in (1.35 m).

Fuselage: semi-monocoque safe-life structure of frames and stringers, mainly of aluminium alloy bit with titanium skinning on the rear fuselage and titanium in areas close to the engine and in some other places; large forward-hinged airbrake under fuselage; reaction-control valves under the nose and in the tailcone.

Tail unit: one-piece variable-incidence tailplane; anhedral 12°; manually operated rudder made of bonded aluminium alloy, as is the trailing-edge section of the tailplane halves.

Landing gear: fully retractable bicycle type, built by Dowty Rotol and designed for rough-field operation; actuation is hydraulic, with compressed nitrogen for single-shot emergency extension; nose unit is a single-wheel (Dunlop 26.00 × 8.75-11) steerable unit of the levered-spring liquid-suspension type, retracting forward; main unit is a twin-wheel (Dunlop 27.00 × 7.74-13) unit of the telescopic oleo-pneumatic type, retracting rearward; outrigger units are single-wheel (Dunlop 13.50 × 6.4) legs of the telescopic oleo-pneumatic type retracting to the rear; Dunlop multi-disc brakes and Dunlop-Hytrol anti-skid system are fitted.

Powerplant: one Rolls-Royce Pegasus vectored-thrust turbofan (exact types listed under Specifications) located in the central fuselage with access through the upper fuselage forward of the wing; each of the four nozzles is of the two-cascade type and rotatable through 98° from the fully aft (parallel to fuselage datum) position; the two low-drag inlets each have outward-cambered lips, and a series of eight suction-relief doors on each cowl aft of the leading edge to provide extra airflow at nil or low airspeeds; fuel is carried in five fuselage and two wings tanks (all integral structures) with a maximum capacity of 630 Imp gal (2,865 litres); additional fuel can be carried in two 100-Imp gal (455-litre) combat tanks or two 330-Imp gal (500-litre) ferry tanks, each type being carried on the inboard pylons; ground refuelling is effected by means of a single point in the rear of the port nozzle fairing, and inflight-refuelling with the aid of an angled probe projecting from the port inlet cowl.

Accommodation: pilot only on a Martin-Baker Type 9A Mk 2 zero-zero rocket ejector seat, in a heated, pressurised and air-conditioned cockpit.

Systems: Marconi-Elliott low-authority three-axis autostabilisation for V/STOL modes; British Aerospace pressurisation system; duplex hydraulic system (pressure 3,000 lb/sq in/207 bars) for Fairey flight controls and other services; retractable ram-air turbine in upper surface of rear fuselage for emergency hydraulic power in the event of engine failure; Lucas gas-turbine starter unit/auxiliary power unit driving a 6kVA alternator for standby and ground-readiness servicing; 1-Imp gal (4.55-litre) Normalair-Garrett liquid-oxygen system; bootstrap cooling system for equipment bay, fed by means of the dorsal inlet.

Electronics: Plessey U/VHF; Ultra secondary UHF; Hoffman Tacan; Cossor IFF; Ferranti FE 541 inertial navigation and attack system (INAS) with a Sperry C2G compass, Smiths air-data computer and Smiths head-up display; Ferranti Type 106 laser ranger and Marked-Target Seeker. The INAS provides visual information via the HUD for the automatic or manual release of free-fall or retarded bombs and for the aiming of rockets and guns, and generally provides the pilot with information enabling him to make first-pass dive and level attacks under most weather and flight conditions.

Armament: the Harrier GR. Mk 3 has no inbuilt armament, but can be fitted with two cannon pods (each containing a 30-mm Aden Mk 4 cannon and ammunition) in place of the ventral strakes; offensive stores are accommodated on one hardpoint under the fuselage, and two hardpoints under each wing, each hardpoint being fitted with an ML ejector release unit; the inner wing and under-fuselage hardpoints are cleared for stores up to 2,000 lb (907 kg) each, and the outer wing hardpoints for loads up to 650 lb (295 kg) each, giving a nominal offensive load of 7,300 lb (3,311 kg). Up to 1982 the Harrier GR. Mk 3 was cleared to operate with a maximum load of 5,000 lb (2,268 kg), but has been demonstrated with loads in excess of 8,000 lb (3,629 kg). Disposable stores can include the following: 100-Imp gal (455-litre) or 330-Imp gal (1,500-litre) drop tanks, 1,000-lb (454-kg) Mk 83 free-fall or retarded bombs, 500-lb (227-kg) Mk 82 Snakeye retarded or LDGP free-fall bombs, 250-lb (113-kg) Mk 81 Snakeye retarded or LDGP free-fall bombs, various types of cluster bomb, various types of rocket-launcher (LAU-10A, LAU-68A, LAU-69A, Matra 155), Mk 77 firebombs, Mk 7 dispensers for APAM clusters or Rockeye clusters, Bofors or Lepus flares, Sidewinder AAMs, Martel ASMs, Harpoon ASMs, and a variety of practice stores.

Right: F402-RR-406, showing the overall similarity to previous generations of the Pegasus despite the fitting of zero-scarf nozzles.

Specifications

P.1127

Type:	V/STOL research aircraft
Accommodation:	pilot only
Armament:	none
Powerplant:	one 11,000-lb (4,990-kg) thrust Bristol Siddeley BS 53/3 (Pegasus 2) vectored-thrust turbofan

Performance:

maximum speed	about 725 mph (1,167 km/h) at sea level
cruising speed	—
initial climb rate	—
service ceiling	—
range	—

Weights:

empty equipped	10,200 lb (4,627 kg)
normal take-off	—
maximum take-off	15,500 lb (7,031 kg)

Dimensions:

span	24 ft 4 in (7.42 m)
length	41 ft 2 in (12.55 m) excluding probe
height	10 ft 9 in (3.28 m)
wing area	185 sq ft (17.19 m²)

Kestrel F(GA). Mk 1

Type:	V/STOL combat evaluation aircraft
Accommodation:	pilot only
Armament:	two rocket-launcher pods, or two 1,000-lb (454-kg) bombs or two 500-lb (227-kg) bombs
Powerplant:	one 15,500-lb (7,031-kg) thrust Bristol Siddeley Pegasus 6 vectored-thrust turbofan

Performance:

maximum speed	660 mph (1,062 km/h) at sea level
cruising speed	645 mph (1,038 km/h) at 5,000 ft (1,525 m)
initial climb rate	more than 20,000 ft (6,095 m) per minute
service ceiling	more than 40,000 ft (12,190 m)
range	150-mile (241-km) radius after VTO

Weights:

empty equipped	11,000 lb (4,990 kg)
normal take-off	13,000 lb (5,897 kg) for VTO
maximum take-off	17,000 lb (7,711 kg) for STO or 19,000 lb (8,618 kg) for normal TO

Dimensions:

span	22 ft 10 in (6.96 m)
length	42 ft (12.80 m) excluding probe
height	10 ft 9 in (3.28 m)
wing area	186 sq ft (17.28 m²)

P.1154RN

Type:	V/STOL high-altitude air-combat fighter project
Accommodation:	pilot and navigator/radar operator seated in tandem
Armament:	four AAMs or bombs
Powerplant:	one 35,170-lb (15,953-kg) thrust Bristol Siddeley BS.100/8 Phase 2 vectored-thrust turbofan

Performance:

maximum speed	about Mach 1.75
cruising speed	—
initial climb rate	—
service ceiling	—
range	—

Weights:

empty equipped	24,300 lb (11,022 kg)
normal take-off	39,400 lb (17,872 kg) for intercept mission
maximum take-off	—

Dimensions:

span	30 ft 6 in (9.30 m)
length	58 ft 6 in (17.83 m)
height	13 ft 3 in (4.04 m)
wing area	287 sq ft (26.66 m²)

P.1154RAF

Type:	V/STOL low-altitude close-support aircraft project
Accommodation:	pilot only
Armament:	missiles and bombs
Powerplant:	one 35,600-lb (16,148-kg) thrust Bristol Siddeley BS.100/8 vectored-thrust turbofan

Performance:

maximum speed	Mach 1.93 at 36,000 ft (10,975 m)
cruising speed	—
initial climb rate	more than 50,000 ft (15,240 m) per minute
service ceiling	52,500 ft (16,000 m)
range	355-mile (571-km) radius on a hi-lo-hi mission with bomb load

Weights:

empty equipped	18,120 lb (8,219 kg)
normal take-off	—
maximum take-off	30,790 lb (13,966 kg) on a low-altitude attack mission

Dimensions:

span	26 ft (7.92 m)
length	56 ft 6 in (17.22 m)
height	12 ft 3 in (3.73 m)
wing area	250 sq ft (23.23 m²)

Harrier GR. Mk 1

Type:	V/STOL close-support and reconnaissance aircraft
Accommodation:	pilot only
Armament:	guns and missiles, rockets or bombs
Powerplant:	one 19,000-lb (8,618-kg) thrust Rolls-Royce Pegasus 6 Mk 101 vectored-thrust turbofan

Performance:

maximum speed	over 737 mph (1,186 km/h) at sea level
cruising speed	—
initial climb rate	40,000 ft (12,190 m) per minute
service ceiling	more than 50,000 ft (15,240 m)
range	60-mile (97-kg) radius after VTO with 3,000-lb (1,361-kg) load

Weights:

empty equipped	12,300 lb (5,579 kg)
normal take-off	21,000 lb (9,526 kg)
maximum take-off	over 25,000 lb (11,340 kg)

Dimensions:

span	25 ft 3 in (7.70 m)
length	45 ft 8 in (13.92 m)
height	11 ft 3 in (3.43 m)
wing area	201.1 sq ft (18.68 m²), or 217 sq ft (20.16 m²) with ferry tips increasing span to 29 ft 8 in (9.04 m)

Harrier T. Mk 2

Type:	V/STOL combat-capable conversion trainer
Accommodation:	pupil and instructor seated in tandem
Armament:	guns and missiles, rockets or bombs
Powerplant:	one 19,000-lb (8,618-kg) thrust Rolls-Royce Pegasus 6 Mk 101 vectored-thrust turbofan

Performance:

maximum speed	as for Harrier GR. Mk 1
cruising speed	
initial climb rate	
service ceiling	
range	

Weights:

empty equipped	13,300 lb (6,033 kg)
normal take-off	—
maximum take-off	over 25,000 lb (11,340 kg)

Dimensions:

span	25 ft 3 in (7.70 m)
length	55 ft 9½ in (17.01 m)
height	12 ft (3.66 m)
wing area	201.1 sq ft (18.68 m²)

Harrier GR. Mk 3

Type:	V/STOL close-support and reconnaissance aircraft
Accommodation:	pilot only
Armament:	guns and missiles, rockets or bombs
Powerplant:	one 21,500-lb (9,752-kg) thrust Rolls-Royce Pegasus 11 Mk 103 vectored-thrust turbofan
Performance:	
maximum speed	over 737 mph (1,186 km/h) at sea level
cruising speed	—
initial climb rate	more than 40,000 ft (12,190 m) per minute
service ceiling	more than 50,000 ft (15,240 m)
range	175-mile (282-km) radius with 4,500-lb (2,041-kg) load after STO
Weights:	
empty equipped	12,300 lb (5,579 kg)
normal take-off	—
maximum take-off	over 25,000 lb (11,340 kg)
Dimensions:	
span	25 ft 3 in (7.70 m)
length	45 ft 7⅞ in (13.91 m)
height	11 ft 4 in (3.45 m)
wing area	201.1 sq ft (18.68 m²)

Harrier T. Mk 4

Type:	V/STOL combat-capable conversion trainer
Accommodation:	pupil and instructor seated in tandem
Armament:	guns and missiles, rockets or bombs
Powerplant:	one 21,500-lb (9,752-kg) thrust Rolls-Royce Pegasus 11 Mk 103 vectored-thrust turbofan
Performance:	
maximum speed	as for Harrier GR. Mk 3
cruising speed	
initial climb rate	
service ceiling	
range	
Weights:	
empty equipped	13,750 lb (6,237 kg)
normal take-off	—
maximum take-off	over 25,000 lb (11,340 kg)
Dimensions:	
span	25 ft 3 in (7.70 m)
length	55 ft 9½ in (17.01 m)
height	13 ft 8 in (4.17 m)
wing area	201.1 sq ft (16.68 m²)

AV-8A and VA-1 Matador

Type:	V/STOL attack and combat fighter
Accommodation:	pilot only, seated on a Stencel SIIIS-3 ejector seat
Armament:	two 30-mm cannon and up to 5,300 lb (2,404 kg) of disposable stores, plus two Sidewinder AAMs
Powerplant:	one 21,500-lb (9,752-kg) thrust Rolls-Royce Pegasus 11 Mk 103 vectored-thrust turbofan
Performance:	
maximum speed	over 737 mph (1,186 km/h) at sea level
cruising speed	—
initial climb rate	more than 40,000 ft (12,190 m) per minute
service ceiling	more than 50,000 ft (15,240 m)
range	175-mile (282-km) radius with 3,000-lb (1,361-kg) load after 400-ft (122-m) TO
Weights:	
empty equipped	12,190 lb (5,529 kg)
normal take-off	17,050 lb (7,734 kg) for VTO
maximum take-off	22,300 lb (10,115 kg) for STO
Dimensions:	
span	25 ft 3 in (7.70 m)
length	45 ft 6 in (13.87 m)
height	11 ft 4 in (3.45 m)
wing area	201.1 sq ft (18.68 m²)

TAV-8B and VAE-1 Matador

Type:	V/STOL combat-capable conversion trainer
Accommodation:	pupil and instructor, seated in tandem on Stencel SIIIS-3 ejector seats
Armament:	as for AV-8A/VA-1
Powerplant:	as for AV-8A/VA-1
Performance:	
maximum speed	as for AV-8A/VA-1
cruising speed	
initial climb rate	
service ceiling	
range	
Weights:	
empty equipped	about same as Harrier T. Mk 4
normal take-off	
maximum take-off	
Dimensions:	
span	as for Harrier T. Mk 4
length	
height	
wing area	

Sea Harrier FRS. Mk 1

Type:	V/STOL multi-role shipboard fighter
Accommodation:	pilot only, seated on a Martin-Baker Type 10 ejector seat
Armament:	as for Harrier GR. Mk 3, plus ability to carry two Sidewinder AAMs; enhanced operational capability as a result of Blue Fox radar
Powerplant:	one 21,500-lb (9,752-kg) thrust Rolls-Royce Pegasus 11 Mk 104 vectored-thrust turbofan
Performance:	
maximum speed	more than 737 mph (1,186 km/h) at sea level
cruising speed	—
initial climb rate	2 minutes 20 seconds to 40,000 ft (12,190 m)
service ceiling	more than 50,000 ft (15,240 m)
range	466-mile (750-km) radius on intercept mission
Weights:	
empty equipped	12,500 lb (5,670 kg)
normal take-off	—
maximum take-off	more than 25,000 lb (11,340 kg)
Dimensions:	
span	25 ft 3¼ in (7.70 m)
length	47 ft 7 in (14.50 m)
height	12 ft 2 in (3.71 m)
wing area	201.1 sq ft (18.68 m²)

YAV-8B Advanced Harrier

Type:	V/STOL attack and air-combat development aircraft
Accommodation:	pilot only
Armament:	two 20-mm or 30-mm guns, plus a maximum of 17,000 lb (7,711 kg) of disposable stores delivered with the aid of an Angle-Rate Bombing System, Marconi HUD and laser/TV target seeker
Powerplant:	one 21,500-lb (9,752-kg) thrust Rolls-Royce Pegasus Mk 804 (F402-RR-404) vectored-thrust turbofan
Performance:	
maximum speed	674 mph (1,085 km/h) at sea level
cruising speed	—
initial climb rate	—
service ceiling	—
range	210-mile (338-km) radius with full offensive load after 1,000-ft (305-m) TO
Weights:	
empty equipped	12,550 lb (5,693 kg)
normal take-off	—
maximum take-off	29,750 lb (13,495 kg)
Dimensions:	
span	30 ft 3½ in (9.23 m)
length	42 ft 10¾ in (13.07 m)
height	11 ft 3½ in (3.44 m)
wing area	230.0 sq ft (21.37 m²)

AV-8B Harrier II and Harrier GR. Mk 5

Type:	V/STOL close-support and attack aircraft
Accommodation:	pilot only
Armament:	one 25-mm GAU-12/U cannon (AV-8B) or two 30-mm Aden cannon (Harrier GR. Mk 5), plus up to 17,000 lb (7,711 kg) of stores on seven hardpoints
Powerplant:	one 21,500-lb (9,752-kg) thrust Rolls-Royce Pegasus 11-21E (Pratt & Whitney F402-404) vectored-thrust turbofan

Performance:

maximum speed	690 mph (1,113 km/h) at sea level
cruising speed	—
initial climb rate	17,400 ft (5,305 m) per minute
service ceiling	50,000 ft (15,240 m)
range	748-mile (1,204-km) radius with seven bombs after 1,000-ft (305-m) TO

Weights:

empty equipped	12,750 lb (5,783 kg)
normal take-off	19,185 lb (8,702 kg) for VTO
maximum take-off	29,750 lb (13,494 kg) for STO

Dimensions:

span	30 ft 4 in (9.25 m)
length	46 ft 4 in (14.12 m)
height	11 ft 8 in (3.56 m)
wing area	230 sq ft (21.37 m²)

Harrier family production

P.1127: six aircraft (XP831, XP836, XP972, XP976, XP980 and XP984)
Kestrel: nine aircraft (XS688 later 64-18262, XS689 later 64-18263, XS690 later 64-18264, XS691 later 64-18265, XS692 later 64-18266, XS693, XS694 later 64-18269, XS695 and XS696)
P.1127RAF: six aircraft (XV276–XV281)
Harrier GR. Mk 1: 78 aircraft (XV738–XV762, XV776–XV810, XW630, XW763–XW770 and XW916–XW924)
Harrier T. Mk 2: 16 aircraft (XW174–XW175, XW264–XW272, XW925–XW927 and XW933–XW934)
Harrier GR. Mk 3: surviving Harrier GR. Mk 1 aircraft upgraded to this standard, and 36 aircraft (XZ128–XZ139, XZ963–XZ973 and XZ987–XZ999) built as new; further orders were placed in 1982 for replacement of Harrier GR. Mk 3s lost in the Falklands Campaign
Harrier T. Mk 4: surviving Harrier T. Mk 2 aircraft upgraded to this standard and eight aircraft (XZ145–XZ147, XZ445–XZ448 for the Royal Navy and civil **Mk 52** registered

G-VTOL for British Aerospace) built as new
Sea Harrier FRS. Mk 1: 24 aircraft (XZ438–XZ440, XZ450–XZ460 and XZ491–XZ500), plus an extra 17 aircraft as replacements and additions after the Falklands Campaign
Sea Harrier FRS. Mk 51: six aircraft for the Indian Navy
Sea Harrier T. Mk 60: two aircraft for the Indian Navy
AV-8A: 112 aircraft for the US Marine Corps (BuAer nos 158384–158395, 158694–158711, 158694–158711, 158948–158977, 159230–159259 and 159366–159377); 61 survivors being upgraded to **AV-8C** standard
TAV-8A: eight aircraft for the US Marine Corps (BuAer nos 159378–159785)
YAV-8B: two aircraft converted from AV-8A standard (BuAer nos 158394 and 158395)
VA-1 Matador: 11 aircraft ordered for the Spanish navy as AV-8S aircraft (BuAer nos 159557–159562 and 161174–161178)
VAE-1 Matador: two aircraft ordered for the Spanish Navy as TAV-8S aircraft (BuAer nos 159563 and 159564)
AV-8B Harrier II: planned procurement of 336 for the US Marine Corps
Harrier GR. Mk 5: planned procurement of 60 for the RAF

Acknowledgments

We would particularly like to thank Mr Lillistone and Mr Shubrook of British Aerospace Aircraft Group at Kingston-upon-Thames for their invaluable help with the pictures for this publication.

Picture research was through Military Archive and Research Services and, unless indicated below, all material was supplied by British Aerospace.
BBC TV News: p. 23 (top left, top right and centre right).
Stuart Howe: pp. 24 (bottom), 40, 43 (top).
Martin Baker Engineering: p. 34.
T. Moore/Military Archive and Research Services: p. 23 (centre left)

MOD (RAF): pp. 24–25, 26 (top), 27, 36–37, 42 (top).
MOD (RN): pp. 23 (bottom), 33 (top), 49 (bottom).
MOD (RN – HMS *Heron*): p. 48 (bottom).
Rolls-Royce, Bristol: pp. 10–11, 28 (top and centre), 46 (top), 52–53.